BUILDING RESILIENCE OF THE URBAN POOR IN INDONESIA

JANUARY 2022

ADB

ASIAN DEVELOPMENT BANK

Contents

Table

Figures

Boxes

Foreword

As the largest archipelagic country in the world, Indonesia has been experiencing severe impacts of extreme weather events due to climate change. Data from the past decade show a significant increase in frequency and intensity of hydrometeorological hazards, potentially disrupting Indonesia's achievement of the various development targets set in the Sustainable Development Goals and its National Medium-Term Development Plan 2020–2024. The Ministry of National Development Planning/National Development Planning Agency (BAPPENAS) estimates that potential gross domestic product loss due to climate change will reach approximately Rp115 trillion by 2024. Urban areas bear the brunt of these losses due to the high exposure of densely populated communities and major economic zones to climate-induced hazards. In fact, a majority of Indonesians now live in cities and the urban population is expected to increase with the country becoming more urbanized.

Despite the economic growth brought about by urbanization, millions of Indonesians still live below the poverty line. The ramifications of the coronavirus disease (COVID-19) pandemic also drew the world's attention to the near poor or those vulnerable to falling into poverty and the new poor. An astute reading of recent country statistics reveals that the well-being and livelihoods of more than 22 million city dwellers are at risk.

Collaborative actions from international, national, and local stakeholders are necessary to mitigate the often-complex risks brought by climate change. The Government of Indonesia's commitment to climate change adaptation is manifest with the recent issuance of the Climate Resilience Development Policy, which by Presidential Regulation No. 18 of 2020 has become part of the sixth national priority in the National Medium-Term Development Plan 2020–2024.

Indonesia is among the three countries included in Advancing Inclusive and Resilient Urban Development Targeted at the Urban Poor, a regional technical assistance project of the Asian Development Bank (ADB). It aims to strengthen the government's capacity in designing and implementing pro-poor investments for building climate resilience. We thank ADB for its support in this initiative and welcome this report as a complement for the Climate Resilience Development Policy 2020–2045. The report furthermore integrates the four priority sectors in Indonesia's policy and identifies pro-poor climate resilience solutions along five priority policy areas: (i) adaptive and shock-responsive social protection; (ii) sustainable livelihoods; (iii) effective public health system; (iv) safe housing; and (v) robust community infrastructure, including recommendations and entry points for building resilience in the Indonesian context.

Our hope is that readers will gain a better understanding of where Indonesia is heading with its climate resilience policy, in particular toward a more sustainable and integrated urban development.

Ir. Medrilzam, MPE, PhD
Director for Environment, BAPPENAS
Jakarta

Acknowledgments

This country report is one of the outputs of Advancing Inclusive and Resilient Urban Development Targeted at the Urban Poor, a regional technical assistance (TA) project of the Asian Development Bank (ADB). The project is financed by the Urban Climate Change Resilience Trust (UCCRTF), administered by ADB with financial support from the Rockefeller Foundation and the governments of Switzerland and the United Kingdom.

The country report was developed under the overall guidance of the Ministry of National Development Planning/ National Development Planning Agency (BAPPENAS), the TA focal agency for Indonesia. The implementation of the TA was led by the Directorate of Environment headed by Ir. Medrilzam who provided strategic guidance during the report preparation and facilitated the consultation process, with support from Sudhiani Pratiwi, Putra Dwitama, and Emod Tri Utomo. The country report significantly benefited from technical guidance provided by Hendricus Andy Simarmata. Representatives of government agencies including BAPPENAS, the Ministry of Public Works and Housing, the Ministry of Environment and Forestry, the Ministry of Social Affairs, the Ministry of Health, and the National Disaster Management Agency also provided inputs during discussions at consultation workshops and meetings. The finalization of the report also benefited from inputs received from participants at the webinar Reducing Poverty and Strengthening Economy through Climate-Resilient Development, organized by BAPPENAS in December 2020.

The country report was prepared under the overall supervision of Arghya Sinha Roy, principal climate change specialist (climate change adaptation), Sustainable Development and Climate Change Department (SDCC); and Yukiko Ito, principal social development specialist, SDCC; with technical guidance and inputs from Joris van Etten, senior urban development specialist, Southeast Asia Department, ADB. Rowena Mantaring (TA coordinator) provided coordination support and Fatima Angela Marifosque (resilience research associate) provided research assistance in finalizing the report. Zarah Zafra and Imelda Marquez, operations analysts, provided administrative support. This report was edited by Kae Sugawara, and the infographic and layout were done by Lowil Espada. Sugar Gonzales, climate change officer, helped facilitate the publication of this report. The report includes photos from Revitalizing Informal Settlements and their Environments (RISE) Program provided by Kerrie Burge, project manager, RISE Program.

The International Institute for Environment and Development (IIED) led the initial drafting of the country report in close consultation with relevant Indonesian government ministries and agencies. The IIED team was led by David Dodman and included the following experts: Rifai Ahmad, Sinta Satriana, Irene Sondang, Diane Archer, Sara Candiracci, Matthew Free, Rachel Slater, Aditya V. Bahadur, Rizqa Hidayani, Gerard Howe, and Yasmina Arief Anshory Yusuf. The country report significantly benefited from background research undertaken on specific topics by Yasmina Arief Anshory Yusuf, Smita Notosusanto, Khair Rangi, Budi Haryanto, and Saut Sagala, and background work undertaken for the wider TA by Joanne Catherine Jordan, Manjusha Rai, and Philippa Keys.

The report benefited from review and comments provided by Shamit Chakravarti, former principal social sector specialist, Southeast Asia Department (currently Country Director, Bhutan Resident Mission); Tiffany Tran, human settlements expert (consultant); John Victor Bottini, social development specialist (consultant), and members of the UCCRTF team: Virinder Sharma, principal urban development specialist, SDCC; and Joy Amor Bailey and Ma. Victoria Antonio (consultants).

Vulnerability to climate hazards. Location and low quality of housing make poor communities more vulnerable to climate hazards.

Abbreviations

APBD	Anggaran Pendapatan dan Belanja Daerah (Regional Revenues and Expenditure Budget or local planning and budget document)
BAPPENAS	Badan Perencanaan dan Pembangunan Nasional (National Development Planning Agency)
BNPB	Badan Nasional Penanggulangan Bencana (National Disaster Management Agency)
DAK	Special Allocation
DTKS	Data Terpadu Kesejahteraan Sosial
ICT	information and communication technology
JKN	Programme Jaminan Kesehatan Nasional (Public Health Insurance)
KOTAKU	National Slum Upgrading Program
MSMEs	micro, small, and medium-sized enterprises
NUSP-2	Neighborhood Upgrading and Shelter Project
PAMSIMAS	Program Air Minum dan Sanitasi Berbasis Masyarakat (Community-based Drinking Water Supply and Sanitation)
PBI	Kebijakan Pembangunan Berketahanan Iklim (Climate Resilience Development Policy)
PKH	Program Keluarga Harapan (Family of Hope)
PNPM Mandiri	Program Nasional Pemberdayaan Masyarakat (PNPM) Mandiri–Perkotaan
PUPR	Kementerian Pekerjaan Umum dan Perumahan Rakyat
RISE	Revitalizing Informal Settlement and their Environments
RPJMN	Rencana Pembangunan Jangka Menengah Nasional (National Medium-Term Development Plan)
SANIMAS	Sanitation by Community
TNP2K	Tim Nasional Percepatan Penanggulangan Kemiskinan (National Team for the Acceleration of Poverty Reduction)

Executive Summary

Poverty and climate nexus needs special attention. Climate and disaster risk poses a serious threat to the socioeconomic development of Indonesia and undermines the country's hard-earned development gains. The risks are expected to increase in the future with climate change, with its widespread impacts on four sectors—agriculture, water, marine and coastal, and health—as prioritized in the *Climate Resilience Development Policy (Kebijakan Pembangunan Berketahanan Iklim,* or PBI) 2020–2045. The major brunt of climate risk will be faced by 26.42 million Indonesians who live below the poverty line and have limited resources and capacity. The climate shocks and stresses will also force the near-poor population hovering marginally above the national poverty line to fall into poverty. Thus, a closer link needs to be established between efforts to reduce poverty and strengthen climate resilience if achievements in both spheres are to be sustained. Poverty reduction interventions, including those aimed at reducing burden, addressing spatial isolation, and improving economic capacity, need to be designed and delivered with current and future climate risk considerations. Climate actions need to be carefully designed so that they explicitly benefit the poor and near poor and do not inadvertently increase vulnerability and inequality. Such a vision is closely aligned with the development agenda of the National Medium-Term Development Plan (Rencana Pembangunan Jangka Menengah Nasional, or RPJMN) 2020–2024.

Explicit focus on building resilience of the poor and near poor in urban areas can ensure that urbanization benefits all equally. Urban areas, comprising nearly 55% of the Indonesian population, are hot spots of climate and disaster risk, with often high exposure and vulnerability to natural hazards. The risks are expected to increase with large numbers of coastal cities facing sea level rise and with high-density built environments resulting in urban heat island effects. Roughly 7% of the urban population are poor, and almost the same proportion just above the poverty line. Often living in slums and informal settlements, in overcrowded housing and with poor quality of basic services, the poor and near poor have to deal with climate shocks and stresses that impact their assets, livelihoods, and limited savings, forcing them to adopt negative coping strategies. In the absence of pro-poor climate resilience actions, such impacts will further increase poverty and inequality. The coronavirus disease (COVID-19) crisis has further exposed the underlying vulnerabilities of the urban poor and near poor and highlighted the urgency to build resilience, especially of the ones most at risk.

Strengthening resilience of the poor in urban areas will require a combination of interventions that collectively promote coping, incremental, and transformational strategies. Climate risk can only be managed by considering the full stream of possible future impacts and adopting a combination of strategies at the appropriate spatial and temporal scale. The strategies should include (i) coping mechanisms, (ii) incremental adaptation to accommodate changes in climate, and (iii) transformational solutions that bring fundamental systemic changes to reduce the root causes of vulnerability to climate change in the long run. These strategies should be targeted at different scales—household, community, cities, subnational, and national—with actions at any scale being complemented by activities and interventions at other scales. Recognizing that the local context often shapes vulnerabilities, decisions to implement such interventions should be based on the principle of subsidiarity; that is, resilience-building decisions are made at the lowest competent level.

Pro-poor national policies and programs provide opportunities to strengthen resilience at scale. Indonesia has robust national policies and programs spread across different sectors and targeted at the poor, including those in urban areas. The country has also identified priority sectors for climate adaptation: water, marine and coastal, agriculture, and health—each of which directly impacts the lives, livelihoods, and well-being of the urban poor. Thus, the design and delivery of pro-poor urban policies and programs can be improved to address current climate risks, especially in the priority sectors, while consciously introducing solutions that capacitate the urban poor households and communities to adapt and transform in the context of future climate risks. This approach not only goes beyond merely reducing harm but also seeks to (i) demonstrate how interventions to build resilience can address the underlying systemic factors in response to climate and its effects; and (ii) improve existing capacity, including acquiring new skills, to prosper in the context of increasing climate and disaster risk.

Five key pro-poor policy areas accompanied with a set of enabling factors provide a framework for advancing climate resilience of the urban poor. Interventions across five priority policy areas—social protection, public health system, livelihoods, housing, and community infrastructure—are critical for securing and sustaining the resilience of the urban poor in Indonesia. Success in each of these areas will be determined by a set of enabling factors: governance, data, and finance. It will also require clarity of the scale and scale-appropriate interventions, ensuring that (i) the objectives, inputs, and activities are aligned with the appropriate scale of impact from households upward; (ii) the principle of subsidiarity (where higher tiers of government share power with governance structures at the local level) is integrated; and (iii) interventions are designed to be scalable and have impact at scale given the size of Indonesia's urban population (Figure 5).

Adaptive and shock-responsive social protection. Social assistance and labor market programs provide important coping mechanisms to poor households in times of shock, including climate-related shocks, and ensure greater human development goals are not compromised. More importantly, such programs also provide the scope to advance transformational adaptation by establishing linkage with building skills, livelihood, and financial inclusion programs that are responsive to climate shocks and stresses. The role of social protection in resilience-building is recognized in the RPJMN 2020–2024, and the Government of Indonesia has initiated a process to develop their Adaptive Social Protection Roadmap. In order to deliver adaptation strategies that benefit the urban poor, social protection systems need both to adapt and remain adaptive to effectively respond to changing climate risks. Actions that can support such objectives include (i) recognizing social protection as an adaptation strategy in national and local climate adaptation policies and plans; (ii) integrating natural hazard, exposure and vulnerability-related data and information in a social protection database; (iii) strengthening the institutional architecture of social assistance programs to allow horizontal and vertical expansion after a disaster and to improve the involvement of local governments in delivery; (iv) exploring the potential of introducing labor market programs that directly support public works in priority sectors of PBI 2020–2045 such as construction of water storage buildings, improvement of residential environmental health, development of nature-based coastal protection, area management and housing, and settlement relocation; (v) aligning financing for social protection programs with the National Disaster Risk Financing and Insurance Strategy and introducing innovative financing modalities such as forecast-based financing; and (vi) raising the awareness of social protection program facilitators on climate and disaster risk.

Sustainable livelihoods. Climate change impacts on assets and capital (natural, physical, financial, and human) on which the livelihoods of the urban poor are based, thus requiring a combination of measures to strengthen resilience, including savings and safety nets; income stability and diversity; education, skills, and mindset; and social network and mobility. Actions critical for promoting resilient livelihoods for the urban poor include (i) introducing targeted policies that allow livelihood programs to reach the poor in the informal sector, including the climate-induced migrants, and capacitating them with new skills that would help them find economic opportunities in urban areas; (ii) exploring the possibility of implementing resilient livelihood programs for the urban poor through local governments and using the Kelurahan Fund; (iii) implementing initiatives dedicated to strengthen resilience of the micro, small and medium-sized enterprises by building capacity for business continuity planning and improving access to disaster insurance; and (iv) introducing disaster-resilient microfinance programs, including the establishment of a calamity fund for microfinance organizations to better respond to their urban clients during climate shocks.

These actions are in line with the RPJMN 2020–2024, which provides a strong policy impetus for livelihood development in the context of poverty alleviation.

Effective public health systems. Climate change is likely to impact the health of the urban poor in Indonesia in many ways. These include heat stress-related morbidity and mortality, and higher incidence of vector-borne and waterborne diseases. There are also potential indirect impacts, such as those that may arise from lack of adequate nutrition due to escalating food prices arising from the impact of climate change on agriculture. Thus, building resilience of the urban poor to the health impacts of climate change is critical. It will require a range of interventions including (i) formulating climate adaptation and health policies and plans that recognize the full spectrum of plausible health impacts of climate change, including heat stress especially in urban areas, and their linkage with other sectors such as food security, and water and sanitation; (ii) increasing the use of climate risk information to inform the design and delivery of health, housing, basic services, and settlement programs, thereby addressing the underlying drivers of vulnerability; (iii) strengthening early warning and surveillance systems that better predict health impacts of climate events and can inform preparedness actions on the ground; (iv) introducing new heat stress-related programs that deliver direct support for urban outdoor workers to address key occupational health and safety issues; and (v) strengthening community awareness through family development sessions included in social assistance programs and new curricula on climate change and health in early education.

Safe housing. Disasters triggered by natural hazards, including extreme weather impacts, can damage the housing of poor households in urban areas due to high exposure to hazards, weak construction, and use of substandard materials. Extreme heat can impact their indoor living condition with their houses not designed to withstand high temperatures. Sea level rise resulting in coastal inundation can reduce the structural integrity of their housing. Thus, strengthening resilience of housing becomes critical and requires a package of measures, including (i) strengthening pro-poor policy on risk-informed upgrading, rehabilitation, and relocation; (ii) instituting climate and disaster risk assessment processes to inform site selection, design of housing, choice of housing material, and the maintenance regime of public housing programs; (iii) strengthening coordination of efforts related to urban land use planning, community- and city-scale infrastructure provision, and housing development; and (iv) promoting housing microfinance to support poor households in constructing resilient new housing, retrofitting existing housing, and conducting repair and reconstruction of housing damaged by disasters. Policies and programs need to recognize that housing and settlements are a social process, with communities at the center. Thus, they need to adopt new models and approaches such as community-led resettlement, land purchase initiatives, and in situ participatory redevelopment for resilient housing, to ensure that the views and priorities of poor households are taken on board.

Robust community infrastructure. Extreme weather events and disasters triggered by geophysical hazards can damage community-level infrastructure such as water supply, sanitation, drainage, waste management, roads, electricity, and community space. Thus, there is a need to ensure robustness of individual infrastructure as part of the wider infrastructure system. It is also essential that such infrastructure promote sustainability, especially source sustainability. In the case of water supply, the source should be sustainable to ensure long-term availability in the face of changing climate. Accordingly, PBI 2020–2045 identifies water as one of four priority sectors as well as the need to develop water storage infrastructures, rehabilitate water catchment areas, apply water recycling and reclamation technology, reinforce regulations on water resource management, and capacitate communities on optimal use of water resources in order to prevent water shortage. Implementing resilient community infrastructure requires moving away from "business as usual" planning and implementation to include measures such as (i) adopting climate-resilient water management approaches such as rainwater harvesting and biofiltration of water, and watershed-level planning at interregional scale; (ii) integrating climate risk considerations in design and implementation of community-based water supply and sanitation programs to encourage behavior change within communities which promotes sustainable and climate risk-informed practices on water management, sanitation, and hygiene; and (iii) promoting green infrastructure as part of programs supporting community basic services. Such actions will support the implementation of RPJMN 2020–2024, which targets the provision of 10 million connections to achieve 100% clean water coverage and 90% sanitation access.

Enabling environment. Enabling resilience actions in specific policy areas requires risk-informed and inclusive governance; climate, disaster, and poverty data; and securing of finance. These factors provide the enabling environment (Figure 5) for securing and sustaining resilience, and they are also critical for facilitating innovation and partnerships needed for scaling up resilience.

- **Inclusive and risk-informed governance.** Governance influences tenure security, access and operation of basic infrastructure and services, delivery of social protection, and livelihood support—all of which have a critical bearing on risk and resilience. The existing framework of decentralized governance in Indonesia provides a solid basis for local action that highlights local needs. However, enhanced coordination is needed at all levels, across agencies and programs, with an explicit focus on resilience, especially since natural hazards have impacts that can cross administrative boundaries, and exposure to hazards may be a result of actions taken beyond a particular administrative boundary. It is also critical to increase the capacity of sub-national, provincial and district/city governments to mainstream climate resilience development as well as to use and apply climate and disaster risk information in preparing their regional development plans and informing decisions for policies and investments. Bottom-up participatory planning processes such as the *Musrenbang* provide a platform to understand the resilience needs and priorities of communities and to strengthen partnerships with civil society organizations.

- **Appropriate and reliable data.** It is imperative that the multidimensional nature of poverty, as well as the range of current and future hazards and their likely direct and indirect impacts are considered when planning, designing, and implementing poverty reduction programs to build resilience. Particularly important is analysis to gain an understanding of the spatial and temporal distribution of hazards, exposure, and vulnerabilities, across a range of scales. This requires climate and disaster risk data produced both by poor urban communities (which capture the local context) and by modern technologies such as earth observation. The use of climate and disaster risk databases such as SIDIK and InaRISK for poverty reduction-related decision-making needs to be strengthened. It is also important to share across administrative boundaries and strengthen compatibility between data systems.

- **Additional and refocused financing.** Financing for urban poor resilience needs to be identified, stimulated, secured, and sustained for impact both in individual interventions and across an ecosystem of urban financing related to resilience and poverty reduction. Such financing has to come from a combination of sources: (i) standard fiscal transfers made to local government, (ii) climate change-related domestic funding sources established by the government, (iii) external grants from bilateral agencies and civil society organizations, and (iv) global climate funds. It should be delivered by a range of appropriate institutions at optimal volume and scale taking into account the principle of subsidiarity. Fiscal transfers such as the Kelurahan Fund need to be strategically utilized to advance resilience in the context of local development. The scope of the Regional Incentive Funds can be expanded to explicitly incentivize climate adaptation. Domestic and international climate finance should be strategically utilized to unlock wider financing for building resilience of the urban poor. Securing and sustaining finances for resilience-building will require long-term technical support for local governments to integrate priorities identified in PBI 2020–2045 in local planning and budgeting.

Recommendations for climate investments in five key strategic areas.
Poverty reduction programs provide a good foundation for building resilience of the urban poor to climate-related shocks and stresses. Some of these programs, with certain degree of adjustment, can help the urban poor cope better with climate risks and, in some cases, even incrementally adapt to the changes in climate. For these programs to facilitate transformational adaptation given the scale of climate risk the country faces, additional investments in five key strategic areas are needed (Figure 9). These strategic areas are aligned with the priorities of the RPJMN 2020–2024 and PBI 2020–2045.

Strengthen awareness on future climate risk for urban poverty reduction.
This includes (i) strengthening awareness among decision-makers; technocrats; local government; utilities; private sector; micro, small, and medium-sized enterprises; financial institutions; and communities on long-term climate risks and their potential implication on the lives, livelihoods, and well-being of the urban poor; (ii) undertaking risk-informed decisions related to the design and delivery of poverty reduction programs, especially those that promote the use of natural resources; (iii) increasing understanding of climate risk at systems levels such as supply chains, to identify cross-sector and multiscale solutions; (iv) utilizing risk information to prioritize spending in specific geographical regions and/or urban areas; (v) integrating climate risk awareness-raising topics in formal education curricula and capacity-building programs for government staff at national and local levels, as well as for communities, especially women; and (vi) aligning various datasets used for poverty reduction programs with climate and disaster risk databases.

Recognize the underlying drivers of vulnerability in climate policies.
This includes (i) factoring climate-induced migration considerations in designing poverty reduction programs in urban areas, especially in the case of social protection, livelihood, and social housing programs; and (ii) adopting innovative approaches, including community-led approaches to address issues of land tenure, which is a key determinant of vulnerability among the urban poor. It is important that national climate policies and plans and priorities for climate finance recognize the importance of addressing the underlying drivers of vulnerability.

Scale up investment in "no regret" or "low regret" resilience solutions.
Such solutions for building resilience of the urban poor reduce the vulnerability to existing and future hazards and perform well across a range of climate change scenarios. Examples include (i) promoting green infrastructure for adaptation as part of urban poverty reduction programs related to basic services, livelihoods, and social protection; (ii) strengthening integrated end-to-end early warning systems; and (iii) promoting climate and disaster risk-informed spatial planning that can help steer growth in a resilient direction.

Invest in selected dedicated new resilience-building programs. This includes (i) employing urban informal workers and climate-induced migrants during lean periods in resilience-building public works programs such as drainage construction, as well as green infrastructure such as protection of coastal mangroves and urban agriculture; (ii) undertaking an integrated program on health, livelihoods, and infrastructure with explicit support for outdoor workers by promoting hydration regimes and outdoor infrastructure to deal with heat stress; and (iii) promoting resilience-building for micro, small and medium-sized enterprises through improved risk information, business continuity planning, and incentive mechanisms.

Enhance financial systems and products to strengthen resilience. This includes (i) strengthening public financial systems to enable appropriate and long-term financing (capital expenditure and operations and maintenance cost) for resilience-building in urban areas; (ii) strengthening systems, including the capacity of urban local governments to access climate finance for implementing priority climate resilience actions; (iii) developing innovative financial products to build resilience of the urban poor, such as through land-based fiscal tools and green bonds; and (iv) developing innovative approaches such as forecast-based financing that allows *ex ante* access to financing for post-disaster response.

Livelihoods are at risk. A large number of the urban poor in the coastal areas are engaged in fishing and vulnerable to the impacts of climate change.

Introduction

Tackling Climate Risk and Poverty Reduction Together to Sustain Results

Efforts to tackle climate change and reduce poverty must come together. Indonesia has made remarkable progress in the last few decades in reducing poverty from more than half the population in 1999 to less than a tenth in 2019. Considerable improvements are visible in life expectancy, access to education, incomes, and basic services. However, the last decades have witnessed development gains being compromised due to extreme weather events, such as floods, landslides, and droughts. Impacts of slow onset hazards, such as sea level rise and water scarcity, are also increasingly being felt. Such impacts are expected to increase with climate change, resulting in intense floods and drought, threatening water availability and health. At a macro level, climate change is expected to impact the Indonesian economy, with losses in four key priority sectors: marine and coastal, water, agriculture, and health. These losses are estimated at Rp115.4 trillion in 2024, which is an increase of 12.76% in the past 5 years.[1] Not surprisingly, the major brunt of the impact will be faced by the remaining poor,[2] comprising 26.42 million Indonesians with fewer and more vulnerable assets, limited access to basic services, and high dependence on climate sensitive sectors for livelihoods.[3] The impacts will

---

[1] National Development Planning Agency (BAPPENAS). 2021. *Climate Resilience Development Policy 2020–2045*. Jakarta.
[2] In this report, poor, as defined by Statistics Indonesia (BPS), is an individual living in a household whose expenditure per person is below the poverty line. It varies by province and type of area, urban and rural.
[3] ADB Data Library. 2021. Basic Statistics, Asia and the Pacific. *Basic Statistics 2021*. 29 April.

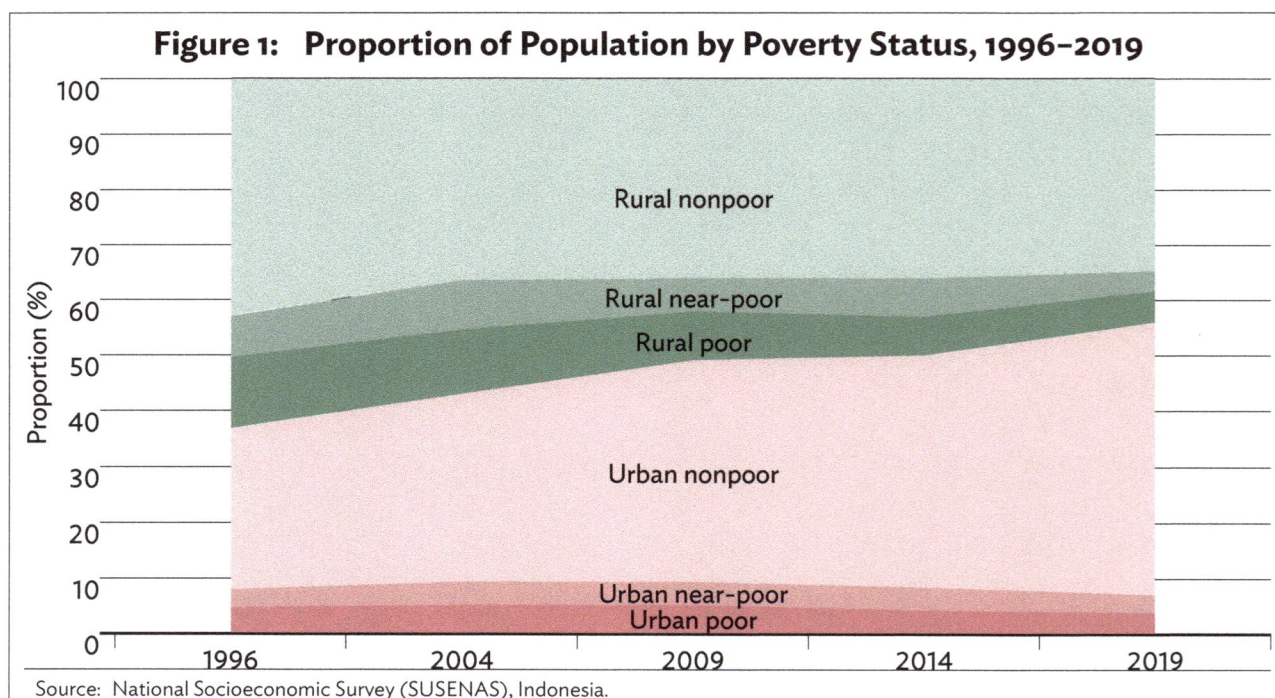

Figure 1: Proportion of Population by Poverty Status, 1996–2019

Source: National Socioeconomic Survey (SUSENAS), Indonesia.

Figure 2: Proportion of Poor and Near-Poor Urban Population (%)

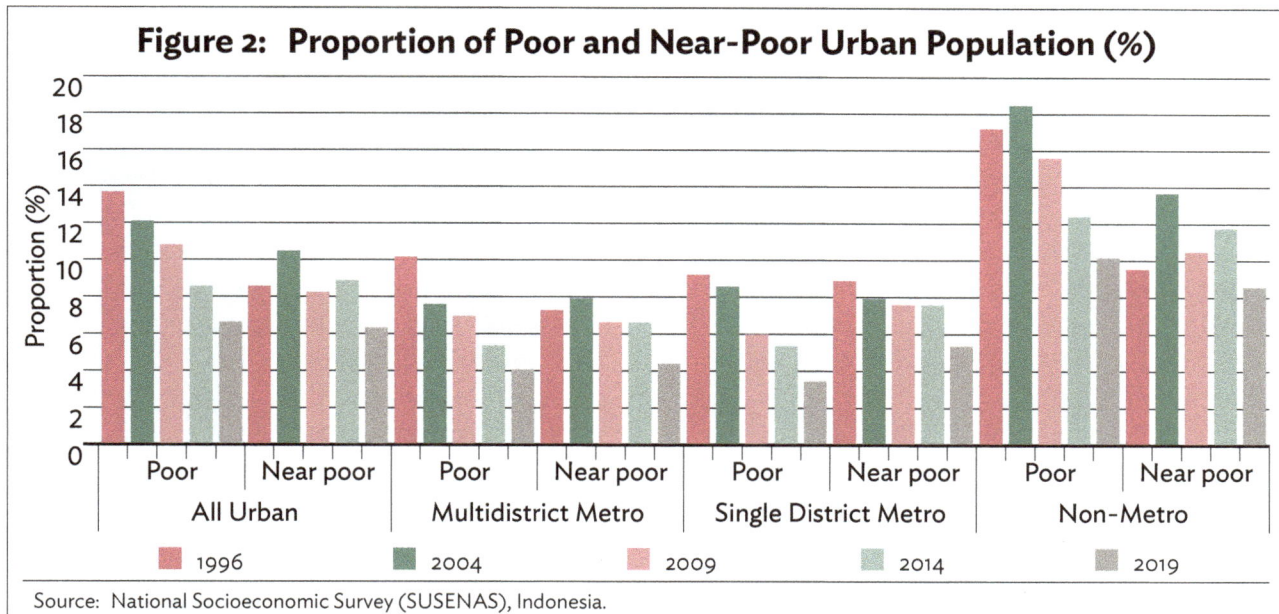

Source: National Socioeconomic Survey (SUSENAS), Indonesia.

also force the near poor hovering marginally above the national poverty line to fall back into poverty, thereby undermining progress in poverty alleviation (Figure 1). Thus, poverty reduction interventions need to be designed and delivered with current and future climate risk considerations. Similarly, climate actions need to be carefully designed so that they benefit the poor and near-poor women and men and do not inadvertently increase vulnerability and inequality.

Climate change adaptation actions require special attention in urban areas, especially those for the urban poor, to ensure the prosperity of urbanization is shared by all. Nearly 55% of the Indonesian population lives in urban areas, with most living in multidistrict metropolitan areas and in non-metro areas. While Indonesia has urbanized rapidly, not everyone has equally benefited from it. Nearly 7% of the urban population lives below the poverty line, and roughly of equal proportion are near poor (Figure 2). Inequality has risen in the country in recent years, with rates higher in urban areas

than in rural areas.[4] With the rising number of urban poor due to urbanization, urban poverty has increasingly become a target of the country's poverty reduction policies.[5] Urban areas are also hot spots of climate and disaster risk, with often high exposure and vulnerability to natural hazards. The risks are expected to increase with large numbers of coastal cities facing sea level rise and high-density built environments resulting in urban heat island effects. The multidimensional nature of urban poverty, typically characterized by reliance on a cash economy, overcrowded living conditions and insecurity of tenure, poor access to basic services, poor health, and dependence on the informal economy,[6] puts the urban poor more at risk. Often living in slums and informal settlements located along riverbanks and in flood zones, with high population density, housing unfit for habitation, and poor quality of basic services, the urban poor have to deal with rapid

[4]   Organisation for Economic Co-operation and Development (OECD). 2019. *Social Protection Policy Review of Indonesia.* Paris.

[5]   World Bank. 2013. Indonesia Urban Poverty and Program Review. Policy Note. Washington, DC.

[6]   D. Mitlin and D. Satterthwaite. 2013. *Urban Poverty in the Global South: Scale and Nature.* London, Routledge.

and slow onset hazards that impact their assets, livelihoods, and limited savings, and force them to adopt negative coping strategies. Moreover, women and men are impacted differently due to preexisting gender inequalities that exacerbate the unequal distribution of existing rights and responsibilities. Thus, in the absence of climate adaptation and disaster risk reduction actions targeted at the urban poor and near poor, such impacts will further increase poverty and inequality and leave more behind.

The coronavirus disease (COVID-19) pandemic has highlighted the need to rethink urban poverty reduction strategies and climate change adaptation actions using a resilience lens. Around 18 months into the pandemic, the highly transmissible Delta variant triggered a second wave of virus outbreak and increased the disparity in vaccine supply across countries, making Indonesia the epicenter of the COVID-19 in Asia[7] as the country recorded more than 3.8 million infection, more than 100,000 deaths, and only 9.33 persons fully vaccinated per 100 population.[8] The pandemic has put almost 10 million Indonesian people at risk of becoming poor.[9] Moreover, the measures adopted to deal with the pandemic—economic shutdowns, physical distancing, and separate vaccination track for corporate employees and their dependents—have exposed the underlying vulnerabilities of the urban poor and gaps in the design and delivery of poverty reduction initiatives. Such restrictions have impacted on both health and livelihood of informal workers who earn income on daily basis. Many of Jakarta's extreme poor are not registered residents of the capital and together with the "new poor," may not have access to social assistance.[10] About 30 million residing in Indonesia's cities are deprived of access to hand hygiene facilities. The congested and unhygienic conditions in slum areas put millions of dwellers at high risk.[11] Most at risk are the urban poor and the near poor being predisposed to live in extreme poverty. The situation has highlighted the pressing need to rethink the design and delivery of poverty reduction initiatives—for infrastructure and basic services, social protection systems, and health—to deal with shocks and strengthen resilience. These lessons should also inform climate adaptation and disaster risk reduction actions in the country.

Resilience at the Center of Reducing Urban Poverty and Tackling Climate

Managing the full stream of future climate risks will require capacity to cope, incrementally accommodate to changes, and most importantly transform systems. Climate change will result in shifting means, tails, and increased uncertainties of climate variables.

The risks can only be managed by considering the full stream of possible future impact and adopting a combination of appropriate strategies at various spatial and temporal scales. The strategies

7 S. Strangio. 2021. Indonesia Bracing for COVID-19 Outbreak to Worsen: Official. *The Diplomat*. 15 July.
8 World Health Organization (WHO). Indonesia: WHO Coronavirus Disease (COVID-19) Dashboard with Vaccination Data. Interactive dashboard (accessed 15 August 2021).
9 ADB. 2020. Social Protection in Indonesia. Discussion Note on Indonesia Country Partnership Strategy.
10 I. Wilson. 2020. COVID-19, Inequality and Jakarta's Urban Poor: Resilient, But at Great Risk. Indonesia at Melbourne. The University of Melbourne. 11 April.
11 J. Etten and T. Tran. 2020. To Survive the Pandemic, Indonesia's Urban Poor Need Economic Support and Help with Basic Services. *Asian Development Blog*.

Figure 3: A Continuum of Adaptation Strategies

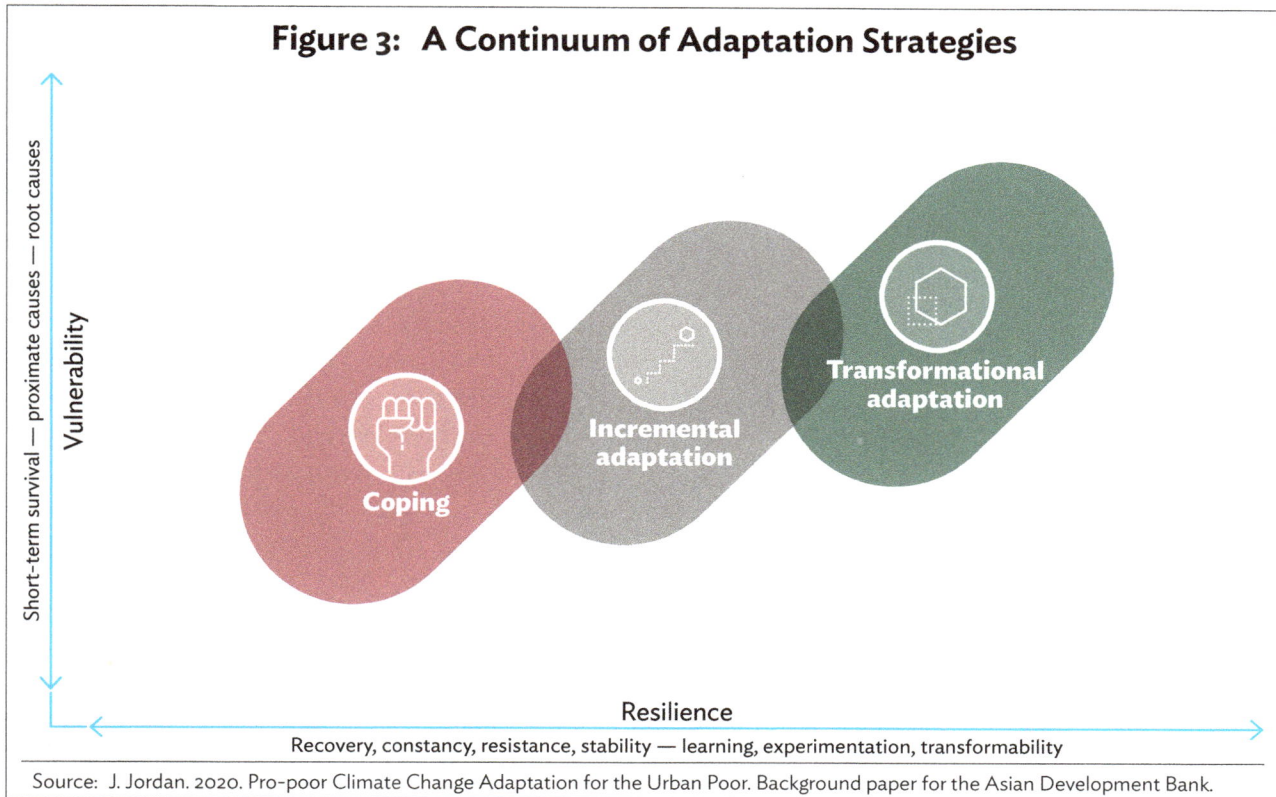

Vulnerability
Short-term survival — proximate causes — root causes

Coping

Incremental adaptation

Transformational adaptation

Resilience
Recovery, constancy, resistance, stability — learning, experimentation, transformability

Source: J. Jordan. 2020. Pro-poor Climate Change Adaptation for the Urban Poor. Background paper for the Asian Development Bank.

(Figure 3) should include coping mechanisms (e.g., stockpiling food for flood seasons); incremental adaptation to accommodate changes (e.g., building higher dikes to protect from increased floods); and transformational adaptation by introducing fundamental systemic changes, which would reduce the root causes of vulnerability to climate change in the long term (e.g., land use changes that introduce nature-based solutions to manage flooding and involvement of local women in protecting such natural resources).[12]

A comprehensive systems approach is needed. Adopting a combination of coping, incremental, and transformational strategies require changes from the urban poor households, communities, cities, and national governments.

First, through the use of robust data and research, they must identify the relevant issues, including how nonlinear changes in weather and climate variables interact with social, gender, economic, political, and cultural factors contributing to changing exposure and vulnerability, which will result in some communities being more at risk than others. Second, they must make decisions based on a good understanding of the effectiveness of possible individual actions at the appropriate level to deal with the issues, including the interdependencies of such actions to ensure they do no harm in the long run and the benefits are equally distributed. And third, they must acquire or promote new capabilities, where needed. It is only with such a comprehensive approach that the urban poor women and men can anticipate, absorb, adapt to, and recover from the impacts of climate shocks and stresses without jeopardizing their socioeconomic advancements—thus, realizing resilience.

12 G. Fedelea, C.I. Donattia, C.A. Harveya, L. Hannaha, and D.G. Hole. 2019. Transformative Adaptation to Climate Change for Sustainable Social-Ecological Systems. *Environmental Science & Policy*. 101. November 2019. pp. 116–125.

A set of planned and/or spontaneous anticipatory actions at different scale are needed to comprehensively build resilience of the urban poor. Building resilience of the urban poor will require planned and/or spontaneous actions that target specific features characterizing urban poverty in Indonesia and thereby reduce the climate impacts faced by the urban poor. These include the following features: (i) urban poor families are largely headed by individuals who are self-employed (footnote 5); (ii) urban poor families are, on average, larger than nonpoor household (footnote 5); (iii) more than 20% of Indonesia's urban population lives in slum areas;[13] (iv) a large percentage of the urban poor population lacks access to safe water; and (v) migration to urban areas is a key strategy adopted to transition out of poverty (footnote 13). Each of these features increases the urban poor's exposure and vulnerability to hazards and therefore should guide resilience-building efforts related to livelihoods, social protection, health, housing, and basic services. Addressing some of these features in the context of climate and disaster resilience might require actions outside urban areas. Thus, a package of actions spread across different sectors will be needed that collectively build the capacity of the urban poor to deal with climate shocks and stresses. The actions need to be targeted at different scales—household, community, cities, subnational, and national—with actions at any scale relying on complementary activities and actions at other scales. Moreover, recognizing that the local context often shapes vulnerabilities, decisions of such interventions should be based on the principle of subsidiarity—that is, decision-making on resilience-building occurs at the lowest competent level, thereby highlighting the importance of local governments in resilience-building. The national and subnational institutions should enable local governments, institutions, and communities with the support needed to make decisions.

Pro-poor national policies and programs with risk-informed and inclusive design considerations provide opportunities to strengthen resilience at scale. Indonesia has robust national policies and programs spread across different sectors and targeted at the poor, including the urban poor, with objective to reduce burden, address spatial isolation, and improve economic capacity. Interventions in these areas typically help address current vulnerabilities and, to some extent, improve the capacity of the poor to cope with different types of rapid and slow onset hazards. In some cases, especially basic services programs, they also help the poor incrementally adapt to the effects of climate change through infrastructure. However, in the face of increasing climate and disaster risk, it is not enough to focus on current vulnerabilities, strengthen coping mechanisms, and incrementally adapt to the impacts; it becomes necessary to consider a full range of future vulnerabilities and, where appropriate, introduce transformational solutions. This is because changes in climate variables will impact the physical and socioeconomic performance of basic services being supported through these interventions. They will also impact agricultural production resulting in increased food prices, which may affect consumption patterns among the urban poor, especially women, increase child stunting, and have longer-term health impact. These effects will stretch the capacity of social protection systems to deal with additional beneficiaries who may have been forced into poverty due to increasing climate shocks; and burden the health systems with increased cases of respiratory and waterborne diseases. Thus, the design and delivery of pro-poor policy and programs need to be revisited to generate wins by addressing current vulnerabilities while consciously introducing solutions that alter the basic characteristics of a system to address the effects of climate change. Doing so in an inclusive manner will ensure the benefits reach all.

---

[13]   Indonesia Investments. 2014. *Poverty in Indonesia: Around 34.4 Million Indonesians Live in Slums.* 3 October.

Figure 4: Impacts of Climate Change on the Urban Poor in Indonesia

Source: Adapted from the Government of Indonesia's Climate Resilience Development Policy 2020–2045 for the purpose of this report.

Priorities reflected in the Nationally Determined Contributions and Climate Resilience Development Policy provide the basis for supporting transformational change in pro-poor urban policies and programs. The Government of Indonesia has committed to supporting climate change control through Law No. 16/2016 on the ratification of the Paris Agreement. As a follow-up to the implementation of the Paris Agreement, the government has submitted its Nationally Determined Contributions with the aim of low-carbon and climate-resilient development. The Nationally Determined Contributions state efforts to achieve climate resilience through economic resilience, social and livelihood resilience, and ecosystem and landscape resilience—which will also influence the urban poor—in accordance with the principle of "no one left behind" by President Joko Widodo in his vision Nawacita. The government recently released its Climate Resilience Development Policy (Kebijakan Pembangunan Berketahanan Iklim, or PBI) 2020–2045, which makes a strong case for scaling up actions in support of climate resilience, especially in four key sectors of the economy: marine and coastal, water, agriculture, and health. Recognizing each of these sectors is critical for strengthening the resilience of the poor (Figure 4), including the urban poor. Climate resilience actions must include an explicit focus on supporting pro-poor policies and programs to improve their design and delivery by integrating long-term climate risk considerations. In some cases, such improvements would imply introducing features that strengthen the coping capacity of the urban poor to deal with shocks and stresses, with incremental changes in design and improvement in implementation capacity, and/or policy shifts that overhaul existing institutions and systems to achieve transformational change.

Climate adaptation finance can play a catalytic role in unlocking the transformative potential of poverty reduction programs to deliver on resilience outcomes. Strengthening the design and implementation of pro-poor urban policies and programs using a resilience lens will require investments in (i) strengthening awareness of the potential long-term impacts of climate risk on urban poverty and urban poverty reduction programs; (ii) ensuring that climate policies recognize the importance of addressing the underlying drivers of vulnerability; (iii) scaling up "no regret" or "low regret" solutions that will generate social and economic benefits irrespective of how the future climate pans out; (iv) developing new dedicated resilience programs to introduce transformational solutions; and (v) strengthening financial systems and products that can unlock future opportunities for building resilience of the urban poor. Such investments can have a positive spillover effect beyond immediate project boundaries and induce additional financial flows from public and private sources to build resilience while reducing poverty. By supporting such investments, climate finance can play a catalytic role for other urban finance streams and support Indonesia in moving toward a resilient urban development pathway.

A Framework for Building Climate Resilience of the Urban Poor in Indonesia

Building climate resilience of the urban poor requires a vision. It envisages that all poor and near-poor households residing in urban areas of Indonesia, irrespective of the differences in gender, age, disability, and migration status, are (i) accurately informed about changing climate hazards and their interaction with changing exposure and vulnerability; (ii) able to factor such information into day-to-day decision-making processes; (iii) better protected from rapid and slow onset hazards through a range of anticipatory across housing, health, infrastructure, and livelihoods, and climate impacts do not reduce their opportunities to improve livelihoods and living conditions; (iv) able to withstand the impacts of rapid onset disasters through improved social

---

Box 1: Vision for Climate Resilience of the Urban Poor Supports Implementation of the National Medium-Term Development Plan 2020–2024

The National Medium-Term Development Plan (Rencana Pembangunan Jangka Menengah Nasional, or RPJMN) 2020–2024 puts forward seven national development agendas. Building climate and disaster resilience of the urban poor is strongly aligned with five of these:

- Agenda 1. **Strengthening economic resilience for quality and just growth**. This supports the need for all Indonesians, including the urban poor, to achieve the basic economic needs that can contribute to their resilience.

- Agenda 2. **Developing regions to reduce inequality and ensure equality**. Inequality is a key driver of risk facing the urban poor, and more equitable regional development will support many of the preconditions for resilience.

- Agenda 3. **Improving the quality of human resources and competitiveness**. Prominent elements are efforts to strengthen social security and accelerate poverty reduction.

- Agenda 4. **Strengthening infrastructure development that supports economic development and basic public services**. Basic services and infrastructure in urban areas are a primary concern. The development of good infrastructure, especially in favor of vulnerable groups such as the urban poor, can accelerate and improve the distribution process of other basic services such as education and health.

- Agenda 5. **Development of living environment to increase resilience to disasters and climate change hazard**. This directly supports building climate resilience.

Source: Government of Indonesia. 2020. Rencana Pembangunan Jangka Menengah Nasional 2020–2024. Jakarta.

protection and emergency services; and (v) able to quickly reestablish conditions for their livelihoods and other functions to flourish because of the continuity of services and access to financing. This vision goes well beyond merely reducing harm; it also seeks to demonstrate how actions to build resilience can address underlying systemic factors in response to climate and its effects and improve capacity, including acquiring new capacities to prosper in the context of increasing climate and disaster risk. Such a vision is closely aligned with five of the seven development agendas of the National Medium-Term Development Plan (Rencana Pembangunan Jangka Menengah Nasional, or RPJMN) 2020–2024 (Box 1).

Building resilience of the urban poor is a process guided by key principles. In considering the resilience of the urban poor, this report highlights the following principles which have been derived through expert literature review and widespread consultation.

- **Building resilience of the urban poor requires actions at different scales.** Poor households, communities, and cities rely on complex infrastructure, social, and political networks if they are to thrive—and actions at any scale rely on complementary actions at other scales.

- **Multiple key policy areas need to work together in a holistic manner to promote coping, incremental, and transformational strategies.** For example, the quality of housing is critical for addressing public health needs (including by reducing the conditions in which communicable diseases, including COVID-19, can spread). Further, cash transfer programs that use poor-quality housing materials as a criterion for eligibility can disincentivize people from improving the quality of their dwellings.

- **Complementarities need to be sought between structural and non-structural solutions.** Nature-based solutions can complement "hard infrastructure" to support the resilience of the urban poor by reducing air temperatures, managing stormwater and flooding, improving urban water supplies, protecting urban coastlines, and reducing wind erosion.

- **Capable, accountable, and responsive governance is critical for coordinating urban resilience, particularly for this to meet the needs of the poor.** Decentralized and responsive governance, with qualified, capable, and adequately resourced local institutions, is critical in this space (principle of subsidiarity). This includes recognition and representation of the urban poor in local development processes (principle of participation) leading to their empowerment.

- **Actions need to be informed by high-quality climate, disaster, and urban information.** The ability to interpret evidence and communicate accordingly to the urban poor is also significant: policy makers need to understand the uncertainty in future climate projections.

- **Improved resilience of the urban poor will require new forms of financing and better alignment of existing finance.** While this may include dedicated "climate finance," the interrelationships between housing, community infrastructure, social protection, and urban development will likely require blending of funds from different sources to contribute to broader resilience.

- **Building resilience of the urban poor creates additional opportunities.** Higher levels of resilience can create new opportunities for the urban poor—informal settler families, other low-income households, and the "near poor"—to improve their health, well-being, and productivity.

Figure 5: Applied Framework for Building Resilience of the Urban Poor

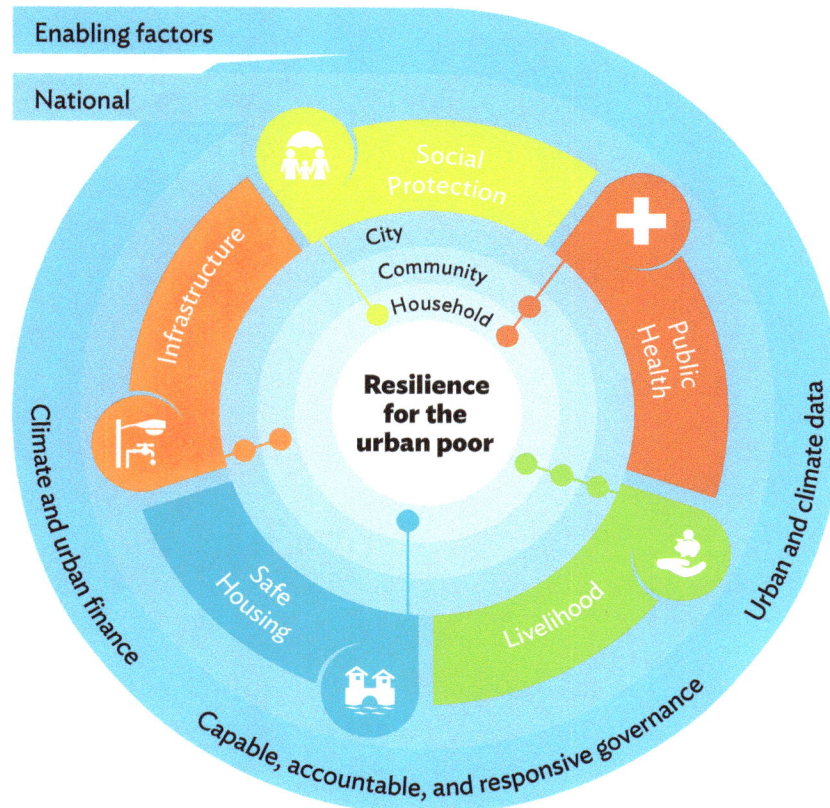

Enabling factors

National

Social Protection

Infrastructure

Public Health

City
Community
Household

Resilience for the urban poor

Climate and urban finance

Safe Housing

Livelihood

Urban and climate data

Capable, accountable, and responsive governance

Source: Asian Development Bank

Building resilience of the urban poor requires a comprehensive framework. Drawing from these principles, as well as an analysis of the context of urbanization, urban poverty, and risk and resilience in Indonesia—including from a changing climate, this report adopts a framework to identify and apply actions to sustainably build the resilience of the urban poor (Figure 5).

Five policy areas than can secure and sustain resilience. This framework identifies five highest-priority pro-poor policy areas: social protection, public health system, livelihoods, housing, and community infrastructure. When these are aligned with climate priorities reflected at national and regional plans, they can secure and sustain the resilience of the urban

poor in Indonesia. Having such a framework enables the identification of opportunities, strategies, and specific entry points within those areas. Additionally, while each area is critical in its own right, each also has important interconnections and interdependencies with the others in the framework. For example, links and complementarities between health and social protection will all serve to increase the impact and sustainability of outcomes.

A set of enabling factors is critical for building resilience of the urban poor. A key opportunity is the rapid expansion of urban areas. This presents possibilities of ensuring that new cities and neighborhoods include the tenets of resilience to ensure that the urban poor are better

Infrastructure plays an important role in building resilience.
Combination of community-level and trunk infrastructure is needed to
build resilience of the urban poor (photo by RISE Program).

able to withstand shocks and stresses induced by climate change. Another key opportunity is to ensure that new climate policies, plans, programs, financing mechanisms, and activities that are proliferating at national and subnational levels speak on the needs of the urban poor to enhance urban resilience comprehensively. Success in each of these areas will be determined by the agents, systems, and institutions that together constitute a set of enabling factors: governance, data, and finance. These factors serve across policy areas, underpinning their success and delivery, for example, ensuring that climate risk and vulnerability data are brought together in targeting interventions or that capability is being built to address resilience at all levels. These factors also require new forms of partnerships. These will need to be (i) within government (including across different ministries and line agencies at the national level, and between local governments and national entities); (ii) between government and nongovernment or civil society organizations, especially grassroots women's organizations that have deep experience and abilities working with the urban poor and promoting community

empowerment; and (iii) between the government and the private sector, which provides many of the goods and services that low-income urban residents require. Importantly these factors address key structural drivers of poverty and vulnerability for the urban poor.

Scale-appropriate interventions and principle of subsidiarity. Success in applying these policy areas, underpinned by enabling factors, also requires clarity on scale and scale-appropriate interventions—ensuring that objectives, inputs, and activities are aligned with the appropriate scale of impact, from the household upward; that the principle of subsidiarity (where higher tiers of government share power with governance structures at the local level) is integrated; and that, given the size of Indonesia's urban populations, interventions are designed to be scalable and have impact at scale.

Where these inputs, enabling factors, scales, and investments are working successfully, the states of resilience and positive outcomes for the urban poor will be achieved.

About This Report

There is a need to identify opportunities to strengthen the design and delivery of pro-poor policies and programs to build climate resilience of the urban poor. While it is recognized that a whole-of-society approach is needed for strengthening resilience, including interventions by individual households, communities, local governments, civil society organizations (CSOs), the private sector, the national government, and the international community, the focus of this report is national government agencies involved in formulating and implementing poverty reduction policies and programs that benefit the urban poor. Based on an analysis of the nexus between climate risk and urban poverty, an assessment of pro-poor policy and programs, and a review of the enabling factors needed to sustain such actions, this report identifies opportunities available to the national government for strengthening climate resilience of the urban poor in Indonesia. The report uses a country diagnostic approach as the basis for effectively informing policy and potential programming decisions of national government agencies in the space of social protection, health, livelihoods, housing, and community infrastructure. The report therefore offers a problem-based approach, rather than a solutions-based approach, to strengthening resilience of the urban poor. This is especially useful, as there are multiple constraints that affect resilience, and this report helps identify the potential levers for change in Indonesia.

Structure of the report. Apart from the introduction and conclusion, the report consists of the following chapters:

- Chapter 2 – **Context**: Describes the nexus between climate risk and urban poverty in Indonesia and agues for the need for targeted yet tailored interventions to strengthen resilience of the urban poor.

- Chapter 3 – **Opportunities**: Analyzes existing policies and programs that have the potential to contribute to resilience of the urban poor. The analysis focuses on social protection, health, livelihoods, housing, and community infrastructure. The chapter provides the core analysis of the report, linking key policy and program areas with their potential contribution to building resilience of the urban poor.

- Chapter 4 – **Enablers**: Explores three key enabling factors that are required to support resilience of the urban poor. The first is the governance arrangements that support the development of policy and the implementation of programs; second, the use and application of climate and urban data, including awareness of and ability to apply these; and third, the financial resources and systems to support programming for building resilience of the urban poor.

- Chapter 5 – **Strategic Investments**: Identifies five key strategic climate investments that can be pursued to unlock the opportunities described in Chapters 3 and 4.

Approach for developing the report. The report was developed following a consultation process with a range of national stakeholders including national government agencies responsible for planning, urban development, climate change, disaster risk management, social protection, and health. These conversations were held to improve the understanding of their needs and challenges in strengthening resilience of the urban poor, including policies, programs, and financing available (or lack thereof) to deal with climate shocks and stresses. Consultations were also held with nongovernment organizations (NGOs) assisting community-led development initiatives to identify good practices and document challenges. Insights were also sought from support institutions to identify their interest and challenges in participating in programs targeted at strengthening the resilience of urban poor. A series of meetings and workshops were an essential component of gathering the information and analysis presented in this report.

Need for Prioritizing Resilience Actions for the Urban Poor

The urban poor in Indonesia are disproportionately impacted by climate and disaster risk. Such risk is expected to increase with climate change and rapid unplanned development. The COVID-19 crisis has further exposed the vulnerabilities of the urban poor. Thus, targeted interventions tailored to address the local context of poverty, inequality, and climate and disaster risk are needed to strengthen the resilience of the urban poor. This chapter makes a case for such targeted interventions.

High exposure to climate hazards. Coastal areas in Cirebon City are highly exposed to flooding and storm surge.

Disproportionate Impact of Climate and Disaster Risk on the Urban Poor

Indonesian cities are hot spots of climate and disaster risk. A combination of factors contributes to this. First, the interplay of economic and physical geography has resulted in Indonesian cities being located in hazard-prone areas along coasts or on floodplains, thereby increasing the exposure of urban population and infrastructure to natural hazards. For example, Indonesia has a vast coastline extending 102,000 kilometers (km), of which 1,800 km are considered highly vulnerable. South Sulawesi Province has the longest most vulnerable coast, reaching up to 573 km (footnote 1). The cities on the coast are at high risk of coastal inundation, coastal flood, and high tides, thereby affecting infrastructure and livelihoods. Second, the pace and pattern of rapid and often unplanned urban development have contributed to increasing exposure and vulnerabilities to natural hazards. For example, urban flooding is a major hazard, and the number of reported floods in 92 Indonesian cities increased 200% from 50 in 2006 to 146 in 2017, due to a combination of reasons including extreme precipitation events,

unregulated urban development, land use changes, deforestation, and land subsidence.[14] Third, the capacity among the different tiers of cities—multidistrict metro, single district metro, and non-metro—may contribute to increased vulnerability and differences in ability to deal with shocks and stresses. For example, rapidly growing non-metro areas or redesignated areas may lack land use and contingency planning capability, infrastructure, economic opportunities, and public funding to effectively manage urbanization—and to invest in resilience.

The urban poor are disproportionately exposed to climate risk. Around 6% of the urban population live in slums, which are often located along riverbanks and canals (Figure 6). Competing uses of the scarce and expensive land available in cities push the urban poor to

14   J. Vun, J. Kryspin-Watson, and K. Simulya Alyono. 2019. *Urban Flood Resilience in Indonesia: New Approaches through an Urban Design Lens*. 17 September. World Bank Blogs.

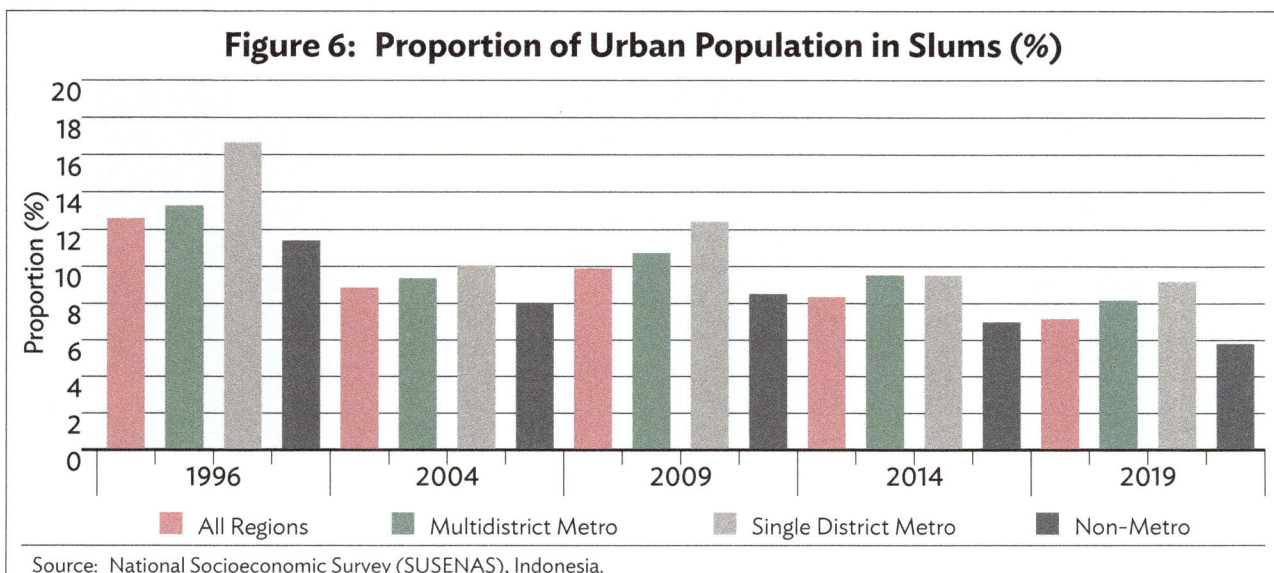

Figure 6: Proportion of Urban Population in Slums (%)

Source: National Socioeconomic Survey (SUSENAS), Indonesia.

Box 2: The Multidimensional Climate Challenges of Cirebon's Urban Poor

Indonesia is widely recognized as a global climate change hot spot of extreme seasonal precipitation and temperature change.[a] Located at a river delta where four rivers meet the Java Sea and inhabited by 333,303 people,[b] the port city of Cirebon ranks as the fourth most vulnerable city to coastal inundation in the East Asia and Pacific region.[c] Approximately 30% (1,100 hectares) of the city's land area is at risk of flooding due to increased rainfall and sea level rise[d] and a more recent analysis classified Cirebon at medium risk from storm surges, when combined with a sea level rise of 0.06 meters and subsidence of 1 meter. Cirebon City has high exposure to humid heat wave, compounded by poor air quality and an intensifying urban heat island.[e] Around 57% of the city population lives in areas highly exposed to multiple climate-induced hazards.

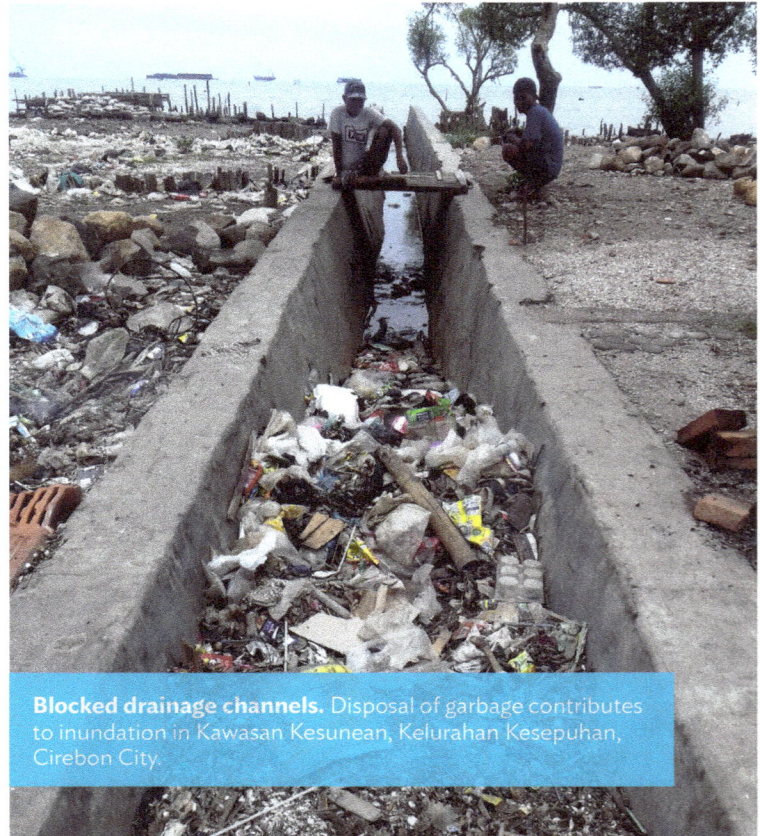

Blocked drainage channels. Disposal of garbage contributes to inundation in Kawasan Kesunean, Kelurahan Kesepuhan, Cirebon City.

In 2017, more than 8,000 households in Cirebon City lived below the poverty line. The urban poor often live in slums and informal settlements. In the lowlands of the city, along the main river and along the coast, there are two slum areas, Trio Cangkol in Lemah Wungkuk Village and Trio Kesunean in Kesepuhan Village, that are highly vulnerable to climate change.

[a] N.S. Diffenbaugh and F. Giorgi. 2012. Climate Change Hotspots in the CMIP5 Global Climate Model Ensemble. *Climatic Change*, 114, p p. 813–822 [Indonesia has amongst the most extreme projections of hot season occurrence early in the 21st century].
[b] Statistics Indonesia. 2021. Population Census 2020.
[c] S. Dasgupta et al. 2009. Climate Change and the Future Impacts of Storm-surge Disasters in Developing Countries. *Center for Global Development Working Paper*, 182.
[d] N.A.H. Pratiwi et al. 2016. Mainstreaming Gender in Climate Change Adaptation: *A Case Study from Cirebon, Indonesia. Asian Cities Climate Resilience*.
[e] M.A. Khafid. 2019. Correlation Analysis of the Impact of Land Cover Change and Ratio Vehicles on the Dynamic of Land Surface Temperature: Case Studies of Cirebon City, Province of West Java. *IOP Conference Series: Earth and Environmental Science*, 399, 012096 [Cirebon's urban heat island has intensified by ~1.2 °C in 20 years].

Lemah Wungkuk is a particularly densely populated area, with 8,576 people living per square kilometer in 2017. Informal settler families live in poor quality and overcrowded housing, lack access to basic services, and have inadequate infrastructure for sanitation, drainage, and solid waste management. Trio Cangkol, in particular, is not connected to the city sewerage network. Although approximately 87% of its households have either a private or shared latrine with a septic tank, 90% of tanks do not meet technical standards and none are desludged (footnote e). Of the households without a latrine, roughly half openly defecate in the sea.

The urban poor in Cirebon City faces complex climate risks year-round. During wet season whenever high tides and heavy rains simultaneously occur, coastal slum areas regularly experience flooding that exceeds 30 centimeters high and lasts up to two hours. Groundwater systems in these areas are at risk of salinization due to rising sea levels and/or drawdown (in land) as well as contamination by foul water. During dry season, these communities are also at risk of intermittent water supply and variable quality during droughts (El Niño episodes), more intense heat wave, and urban heat island episodes (especially at night). The discharge of blackwater directly into the environment, through open defecation and overflowing septic tanks, not only presents a daily health hazard among residents who use the seawater for bathing and washing but may also cause potential spread of diseases during episodes of flooding and heat wave.

To further compound these challenges, coastal slum residents have been reclaiming land by building on the river delta's natural sedimentation using layers of solid waste. Residents either sell these plots of new land for profit or construct homes on them, thereby perpetuating environmental degradation and increasing climate risk.

Climate-related shocks and stresses disproportionately impact the well-being and limited assets of the urban poor in Cirebon City. The multidimensional urban and climate challenges, thus make it an especially urgent opportunity for innovative and targeted solutions for urban resilience.

Source: Asian Development Bank

Solid waste used for reclamation. Solid waste is used by coastal slum residents of Kawasan, Kelurahan Kesepuhan, Cirebon City, to reclaim land along the river delta. This exposes them to hazards and increases climate risk.

Informality contributes to climate vulnerability. Self-employed workers in the informal economy lack access to job-related benefits and are more susceptible to job loss and shortage of earnings - limiting the ability of their households to respond to climate hazards.

occupy hazard-prone areas that put their lives, livelihoods, and assets at risk from the impacts of disasters. Box 2 describes the high risk faced by residents of the slum areas of Cirebon City. Similarly, Jakarta residents are highly exposed to tidal flooding, storm surges, and sea level rise compounded by the city's location, much of it being below sea level. The highest incidence of poverty and flooding is recorded in north Jakarta, increasing the risk for slum dwellers. Recurrent flooding can disrupt and possibly cause loss of livelihoods and assets; contaminate drinking water; and spread diseases (footnote 5). Some of the most urbanized regions of the country such as Sumatra, Sulawesi, Bali, and Java also have a high exposure to precipitation-induced landslides.[15] The poor make up a majority of those exposed as they occupy unstable hill slopes in densely populated cities due to skyrocketing prices of safer land.

Poverty and informality contribute to climate vulnerability. While not all people working in the urban informal economy or living in informal settlements are poor, there is a high degree of overlap. Lack of financial resources, paucity of safe housing, lack of risk-informed urban planning, inadequate access to basic services, and poor governance and accountability structures directly limit the ability of individuals to respond to rapid and slow onset hazards. Urban poor families are largely headed by individuals who are self-employed in the informal economy and thus more susceptible to job loss, shortage of household earnings, and lack of access to job-related benefits (footnote 5). However, workers engaged in the informal economy are key for supporting the functioning of the formal economy, as seen in the case of Jakarta's vast population living in informal settlements and engaged in informal employment or work as household help, security guards, and in small businesses such as food stalls and retail kiosks.[16] In addition, almost 2 of every 10 urban Indonesians live in informal settlements with limited access to basic services such as water supply, sanitation, adequately spaced roads, and open spaces.

Poverty, informality, and adaptive capacity. Informality is not just about informal built environments or engagement in the informal economy. It is equally about the way of life of the urban poor and thus, where appropriate, should be tapped as a strategy for building resilience. For example, many low-income urban residents have a strong awareness of local hazards and are constantly developing solutions—raising homes, changing livelihoods—to cope with increasing climate and disaster risk. Often, strong informal social and economic networks are found within the informal settlements. These networks support one another through community savings groups, early warning systems, and small-scale civil works, which contribute to the adaptive capacity of the poor households. However, the sharp increase in climate and disaster risk requires actions to harness such local capacity. In some cases, increasing

15   J. Cepeda, H. Smebye, B. Vangelsten, F. Nadim, and D. Muslim. 2010. *Landslide Risk in Indonesia*. Global Assessment Report on Disaster Risk Reduction. Geneva: United Nations.

16   World Bank. 2011. Mayor's Task Force on Climate Change. *Disaster Risk and the Urban Poor*. Jakarta.

Figure 7: Historic and Projected Average Annual Temperature in Indonesia under Two Emissions Pathways Estimated by the Model Ensemble

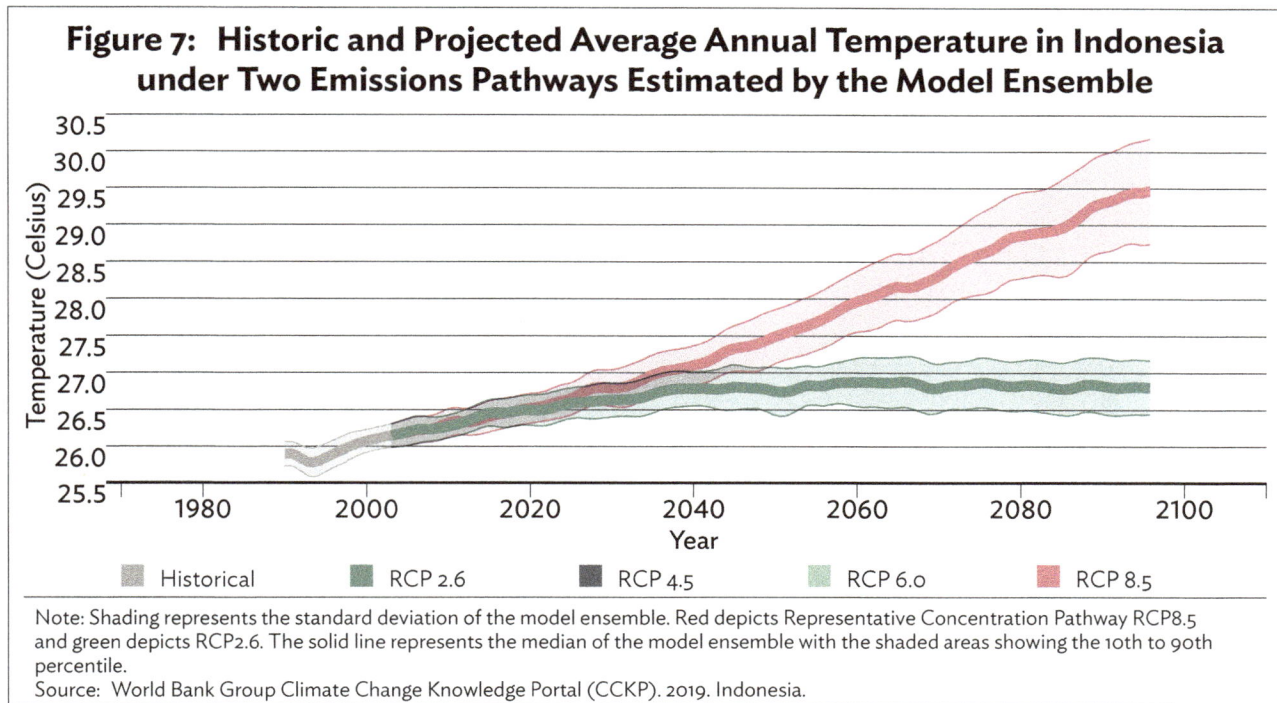

Note: Shading represents the standard deviation of the model ensemble. Red depicts Representative Concentration Pathway RCP8.5 and green depicts RCP2.6. The solid line represents the median of the model ensemble with the shaded areas showing the 10th to 90th percentile.
Source: World Bank Group Climate Change Knowledge Portal (CCKP). 2019. Indonesia.

climate risk also affects poor households' behavior, including selection of low-risk but low-return livelihood options, which further reduces their capacity to manage risks. For example, an increase in tidal flooding has compelled many fishpond farmers in the north coast of Java to switch to informal jobs with less income.

Structural inequalities contribute to multidimensional vulnerabilities. In addition to income poverty, structural inequalities such as gender norms, social rules, class, exclusion, and uneven power relations all intersect to contribute to multidimensional vulnerabilities of the urban poor. Women in Indonesia are poorer at almost all ages than men, and the disadvantages they face relative to men are compounded over the course of the life cycle (footnote 4). Households headed by women are often more vulnerable and have limited capacity to invest in resilience because of the discrimination they face in the labor market, both in terms of employment opportunities and wages. Being single parents, they also face the double burden of caregiving and having to work for a living.

Diversity among the urban poor creates differentiated vulnerabilities. The urban poor are not a homogenous group. Residents come from a variety of different sociocultural backgrounds, which can result in complex power dynamics within and between groups. The diversity of the urban poor also creates differentiated vulnerabilities, based not only on their age, health, presence of disability, ethnicity, and gender, but also security of income, tenure status (including whether a renter or structure owner), levels of education, and familiarity with and length of residence in the city with large numbers having migrated from rural areas.

Future climate will have significant impact on urban areas. Future climate, including increase in temperature, change in precipitation, sea level rise, and increase in intensity and frequency of extreme weather events will directly impact the lives, livelihoods, and health of the urban poor:

Figure 8: Proportion of Population in Urban Areas (%)

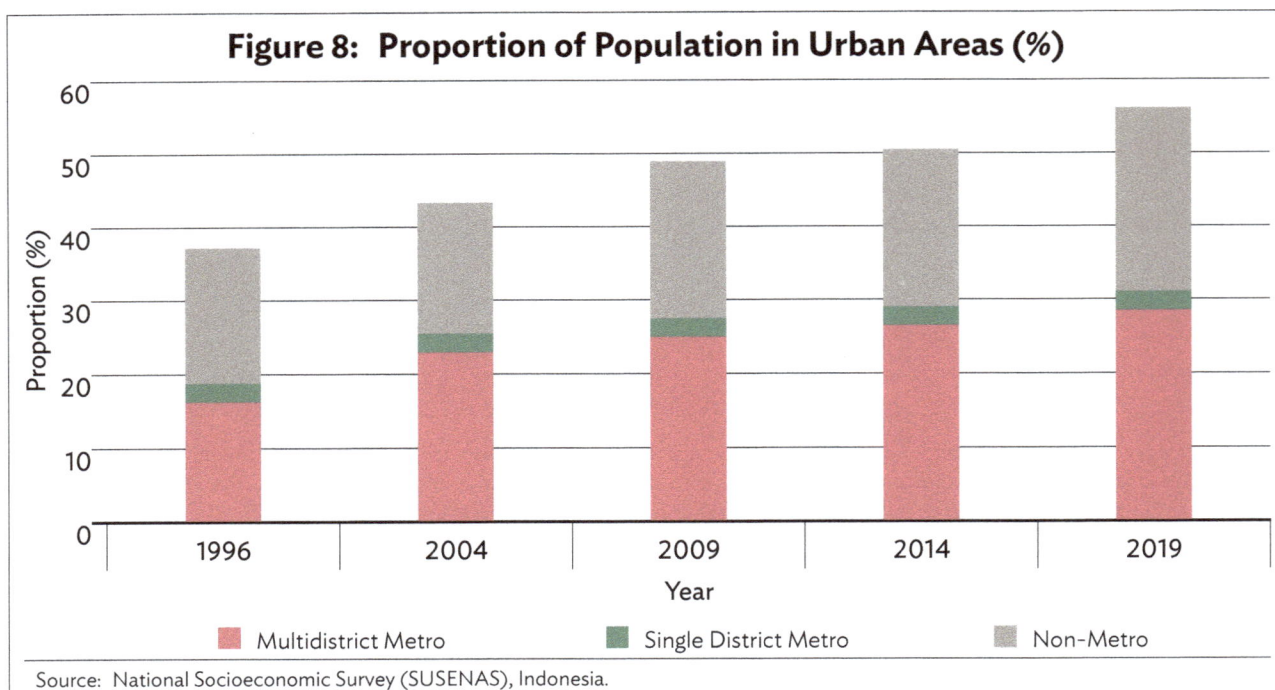

Source: National Socioeconomic Survey (SUSENAS), Indonesia.

- Projections for annual average temperature rise for Indonesia is 3.4°C under the Representative Concentration Pathway (RCP) RCP8.5 emissions pathway by 2080 through year 2100 (Figure 7).[17] Warming projections suggest a rise of ambient temperatures from approximately 26.5°C to 29°C–30°C, significantly increasing the frequency of days with temperatures over 30°C. Significantly higher rates of warming may be experienced in Indonesia's inland regions.[18] For example, warming by year 2100 under RCP8.5 approaches 4°C over the central regions of Kalimantan and Sumatra.

- The effects of rising temperature and heat stress are increasingly being intensified by the occurrence of urban heat island. Studies show how land use changes associated with urbanization in Indonesia have resulted in urban heat island effects, especially in the capital Jakarta.[19]

- Temperature rise is expected to impact water availability. Water scarcity has been projected to happen over the 2020–2034 and 2030–2045 periods. In 2024, the average decrease in Java Island will reach 439.21 cubic meters per capita per year (m³/capita/year) and 1,098.08 m³/capita/year in Nusa Tenggara (footnote 1).

- Floods are a significant hazard in the country, and estimates suggest a 75% increase in population exposed to river flood risk between 2015 and 2055 (footnote 12). The increase in intensity of rainfall will exacerbate existing drainage problem and flooding in urban areas. A recent study estimates that the yearly cost

[17] World Bank Group Climate Change Knowledge Portal (CCKP). 2019. Indonesia. Interactive Dashboard.
[18] KNMI. 2019. Climate Explorer: CMIP5 Projections.

[19] L. Tursilowati, J. Tetuko, J. Sri Sumantyo, H. Kuze, and E. Adiningsih. 2012. Relationship between Urban Heat Island Phenomenon and Land Use/Land Cover Changes in Jakarta – Indonesia. *Journal of Emerging Trends in Engineering and Applied Sciences*. 3 (4). pp. 645–653.

Exposure to climate hazards. Informal houses along the coast of Kelurahan Kebonbaru, Cirebon City are exposed to floods and sea level rise.

of flood damage in Jakarta will go up by 322% to 402% by 2050.[20]

- Sea level rise is projected to reach 35–40 centimeters (cm) in 2050, relative to the year 2000, and up to a maximum of 175 cm by year 2100.[21] It is estimated that sea level rise will submerge 2,000 of the country's smaller islands by the middle of the century and that coastal flooding will affect 5.9 million people annually by year 2100.[22] A sea level rise of 50 cm, coupled with land subsidence in Jakarta Bay, could permanently submerge densely populated areas of Bekasi and Jakarta with more than 270,000 residents.[23]

- The increase in temperature and rainfall can trigger the source of vector-borne disease, particularly the *Aedes* sp. mosquitoes. An assessment carried out by the Ministry of Health shows that diseases such as malaria and pneumonia will also increase due to climate change. The occurrence of dengue hemorrhagic fever will be very high in Pekanbaru, Palembang, Banjarbaru, Banjarmasin, Samarinda, Tarakan, Kolaka, Ambon, Semarang, and Kupang (footnote 1).

- Changes in climate patterns can increase rural-to-urban and urban-to-urban migration in the country.

---

[20] N. Fajar Januriyadi. 2020. Jakarta's Flood Costs Will Increase by up to 400% by 2050, Research Shows. The Conversation. 11 January.

[21] BAPPENAS. 2013. *National Action Plan for Climate Change Adaptation (RAN-API) Synthesis Report.* Jakarta: Ministry of National Development Planning of the Republic of Indonesia.

[22] United States Agency for International Development (USAID). 2017. *Climate Risk Indonesia.* Washington, DC.

[23] Deltares. 2018. *Baseline Analysis of Urban Flood Risk and High Priority Investment Gaps in Indonesian Cities. Technical Report.* Washington, DC: World Bank.

Explicit Actions Needed for Building Resilience of the Urban Poor

Explicit focus on the poor and near poor is needed to deal with climate risk in urban areas. Indonesia is the fastest urbanizing country in Asia. Urban areas in the country are growing at 4.4% per year. By 2025, 68% of the country will live in towns or cities, and this number will rise to more than 73% by 2030 (Figure 10).[24] In 2010, cities accounted for over 44% of the country's non-petroleum gross domestic product (GDP). Cities and towns also accounted for 86% of the 21 million jobs generated from 2001 to 2011—of which 17 million or 94% were in the services sector, showing a significant shift in the employment base.[25] Yet, Indonesia is not benefiting from all the positive returns to urbanization for many reasons that include increase in disaster risk (footnote 24). If not planned well, this rapid urban growth will result in an increase in exposure and vulnerability of the urban infrastructure and population to climate and disaster risk. With the absolute number of urban poor expected to increase and their high levels of vulnerability, it is increasingly important to explicitly target the urban poor for Indonesia's resilience-building efforts. This case is further strengthened by the fact that additional 7% of the country's urban population are "near poor" and in constant danger of dipping into poverty, including from shocks related to climate and disaster. In the absence of explicit interventions to strengthen resilience, efforts to eradicate remaining poverty will not be achieved and even undermine poverty reduction achievements to date.

COVID-19 has further highlighted the need to focus on resilience of the urban poor. The COVID-19 pandemic has required a fundamental reassessment of the nature of risk and resilience around the world, with specific implications for urban areas. The most significant outbreaks of the disease have taken place in towns and cities, and the social and economic implications of so-called lockdowns have been felt most severely in these settings. For example, many poor neighborhoods in north Jakarta have limited access to clean water and sanitation and depend on buying water from vendors, which will be difficult during lockdowns (footnote 10). A variety of factors make virus transmission more likely and strategies to address it more challenging in urban poor neighborhoods.[26] These include high population density, limited income and savings, and high-risk work environments, among others. A large percentage of Jakarta's population reside in crowded *kampung* and slums, where residents live in dwelling units with average size of 9 square meters and frequently share facilities for cooking and washing (footnote 10). In addition, a range of systemic factors make certain subgroups among the urban poor particularly vulnerable, including people with disabilities who may be less able to self-isolate; gendered impacts with the potential for increased care burdens for women and girls, and the potential for increased rates of gender-based violence under quarantine conditions; and migrant workers who may be living far from home without access to social safety nets.[27] In addition, the experience of COVID-19 highlights the further potential for major infectious disease pandemics

---

[24] World Bank. 2016. Indonesia's Urban Story.
[25] B.D. Lewis. 2013. Urbanization and Economic Growth in Indonesia: Good News, Bad News and (Possible) Local Government Mitigation. https://www.tandfonline.com/doi/abs/10.1080/00343404.2012.748980.

[26] D. Mitlin. 2020. Dealing with COVID-19 in the Towns and Cities of the Global South. *International Institute for Environment and Development blog.* 27 March.
[27] A. Wilkinson. 2020. Local Response in Health Emergencies: Key Considerations for Addressing the COVID-19 Pandemic in Informal Urban Settlements. *Environment and Urbanization.* 32 (2). pp. 503–522.

to have lasting implications on the well-being and resilience of the urban poor. Moreover, future pandemics or other related shocks may overlap with climate and disaster-related events which are likely to occur more frequently. Thus, the responses to the current pandemic and the measures that are put in place will shape the likelihood for and implications of subsequent disease outbreaks.

Explicit interventions need to be tailored to address the local context of poverty, inequality, and climate risk. Urban growth and urban poverty profiles vary by tiers of cities in Indonesia. The proportion of the poor and near poor are particularly high in non-metro areas, with close to 10% of population being poor and more than 8% population near poor. More than 30% and 35% of the urban poor in non-metro areas do not have access to safe water supply and sanitation facilities, respectively. Urban poverty

also varies by region. For example, the urban poverty rate is under 4.7% in Kalimantan but 24% in Nusa Tenggara (NT), with regions such as Java and Sumatra falling somewhere in the middle at about 9.6% and 11.6%, respectively (footnote 5). Therefore, interventions to reduce urban poverty whose design is based on the national average may not work. In addition, poverty reduction focusing solely on reducing income poverty may not always be the solution; social and cultural issues need to be considered.[28] Similarly, climate impacts are likely to vary with location and with seasons. For example, with climate change, annual precipitation is expected to increase across the majority of the islands, except in southern Indonesia where it is projected to decline by up to 15%. Impacts may also vary in different seasons. Some parts of Borneo and

---

[28] W.R. Jati. 2019. *How Can Indonesia Eliminate Its Endemic Poverty?* World Economic Forum. 21 August.

Tailored approach to build resilience. The location and multidimensional nature of poverty in informal settlements should be considered when developing a tailored approach to resilience-building.

Sumatra may likely become wetter by 10%–30% during December–February by the 2080s.[29] Estimates suggest that the potential losses from climate change in terms of per capita income by province vary by around 1%–5%.[30] Losses in urban areas will be primarily due to impacts of sea level rise on infrastructure and due to climate-related health impacts. Therefore, building resilience of the urban poor requires a tailored approach based on a granular understanding of the local context driving poverty, inequality, and climate and disaster risk.

Strong national government leadership is needed to scale up explicit efforts to build climate resilience of the urban poor. Recognizing the scale of the dual issues—urban poverty and climate change—and the urgency to act, it is imperative that the Government of Indonesia scale up actions that explicitly build the resilience of the urban poor by promoting a combination of appropriate coping, incremental, and transformational strategies. Such actions need to work in tandem with actions for building resilience of the rural poor. Strong leadership of the government will specifically be required to promote transformative adaptation, which may require reconciling a different future vision for urban development (such as economic growth vs.

equitable and resilient growth); overcoming social and political barriers, as well as power imbalances; ensuring more resources; and involving multiple stakeholders across levels. Implementing such strategies will mean inducing shifts in urbanization policy, approaching existing urban poverty reduction programs with a resilience lens, and improving the factors that would enable such actions to sustain. Such actions by the national government will eventually help overcome barriers faced by local governments, poor communities, and poor households to strengthen resilience and unlock the potential for adopting a whole-of-society approach for tackling climate change and reducing poverty. This will directly contribute to the priorities of PBI 2020–2045, including improved human resource development by focusing on poverty alleviation, social protection, and health; urban infrastructure development by improving access to decent, safe, affordable housing and settlements, and decent and safe drinking water and sanitation; and strengthened disaster preparedness. It will also contribute to the new normal in the post-COVID-19 world, which recognizes the importance of well-being and inclusiveness, improving supply chain resilience and the circular economy, and fostering behavior change.

[29] World Bank Group Climate Change Knowledge Portal (CCKP). Indonesia Projections.
[30] USAID. 2016. *Indonesia: Costs of Climate Change 2050*. Technical Report. Washington, DC.

Securing and Sustaining Resilience of the Urban Poor

Securing and sustaining resilience of the urban poor requires a package of complementary interventions in different sectors and across different scales. These interventions collectively should help address current vulnerabilities while building the capacity of the poor and vulnerable population to deal with future vulnerabilities in the context of changing climate. While increasing the capacity to cope and incrementally adapt, these interventions should promote transformational change in order to address the underlying drivers of vulnerability. This chapter discusses five policy areas that need to work together at different scales (household, community, and cities) to achieve the vision of resilient urban poor households in Indonesia.

Nature-based solutions. The RISE pilot in Batua community in Makassar showcases the use of nature-based solutions for sanitation and flood risk reduction (photo by RISE Program).

Resilience through Adaptive and Shock-Responsive Social Protection

Climate impacts may compromise human development goals. The urban poor are disproportionately exposed to various shocks and stresses, including the ones triggered by natural hazards and climate change, the effects of which result in loss or disruption of livelihoods and loss of income. In many cases, these effects may require the urban poor to adopt negative coping strategies, including reducing consumption levels, incurring high levels of indebtedness, and removing children from school, and other strategies that may affect their long-term well-being and exacerbate their poverty. The Government of Indonesia placed social protection at the heart of its inclusive growth strategy, with the National Medium-Term Development Plan (RPJMN) for 2020–2024 emphasizing the need to redesign existing social protection schemes and integrate social assistance subsidies to achieve program complementarity, faster distribution of social assistance, better targeting and outcomes, and improve beneficiary welfare. The role of social protection in resilience-building is also recognized in the RPJMN 2020–2024, and the government has initiated a process to develop an adaptive social protection road map.

The improvements to routine social protection can strengthen household capacity to anticipate and absorb the impacts of hazard-related shocks (*ex ante*), as well as to support in effective post-disaster response and recovery of the well-being of the poor households (*ex post*). Both elements are integral to adaptive social protection and, taken together, can help make the urban poor households resilient to climate and disaster risk. Social protection programs with their key instruments in Indonesia, such as regular cash assistance and asset transfer, can provide additional protection and complementary support to address the vulnerabilities faced by individuals and poor households and to build resilience of the urban poor by tackling the root causes of vulnerability. For example, social protection programs can support a combination of adaptation strategies by reducing vulnerability which can *protect* household consumption, ensuring that people stay well-nourished in the event of a shock, such as floods; *prevent* negative coping strategies where households do something that allows them to cope in the short term to deal with stresses such as drought but that has a negative effect on them in the long term such as selling productive assets or removing children from school; *promote* the building of human, physical, and financial assets that support improved livelihoods; and *transform* the social and economic drivers of deprivation and exclusion that keep poor people poor.

Indonesia has been an international leader in developing its social registry. The Data Terpadu Kesejahteraan Sosial (DTKS) (previously known as the Unified Database) is now housed in the Ministry of Social Affairs that contains a list of the poorest 40% of households in the country and is transitioning away from relative rankings of poverty toward absolute measures.[31] The DTKS has been used by social assistance programs including Sembako, PKH, Penerima Bantuan Iuran Jaminan Kesehatan Nasional (PBI-JKN), and Programme Indonesia Pintar (PIP) to generate lists of potential beneficiaries. The registry is not exclusively used by all programs for eligibility determination, identification, and enrollment, and some programs also use other databases to generate lists of potential beneficiaries (footnote 30). However, each social protection program has created a number of parallel information systems, which span issues such as assessing needs and

---

[31] World Bank. 2020. *Investing in People: Social Protection for Indonesia's 2045 Vision.* Jakarta

eligibility, making decisions on eligibility and enrollment, determining benefit levels, monitoring conditionality, ensuring compliance, administering and delivering payments, and managing grievances (footnote 30). There are ongoing efforts to establish a full and integrated approach to data management such as through the Sistem Informasi Kesejahteraan Sosial-Next Generation (SIKS-NG), which consolidates information from social protection programs and others programs, in combination with the DTKS. At present there is no interface between DTKS and climate and disaster risk databases (such as SIDIK and InaRISK) maintained by other national agencies that would be essential for climate and disaster risk-informed targeting for the urban poor.

Several social assistance programs provide support to poor Indonesians, predominantly in the form of cash transfers. Social assistance payments are made primarily through bank accounts, which used to be largely delivered in person. The Rastra program, which provided subsidized rice for poor households, was transformed in 2017 into non-cash food assistance program (Bantuan Pangan Non Tunai, BPNT) to provide the beneficiaries with family welfare debit cards (Kartu Keluarga Sejahtera – KKS) that can be used at authorized shops (e-warongs) that sell food commodities. In 2020, BNPT was further transformed into the Sembako Program by increasing the number of food items and expanding the number of beneficiaries to 18.8 million as of 2021.[32] Indonesia's flagship conditional cash transfer program is Program Keluarga Harapan (PKH, Family of Hope), which aims to improve human capital by providing cash transfers to 10 million households on the condition that they access specific health and education services. The Programme Indonesia Pintar (PIP) supports 19.7 million school-age children from poor and vulnerable families to cover some of the personal

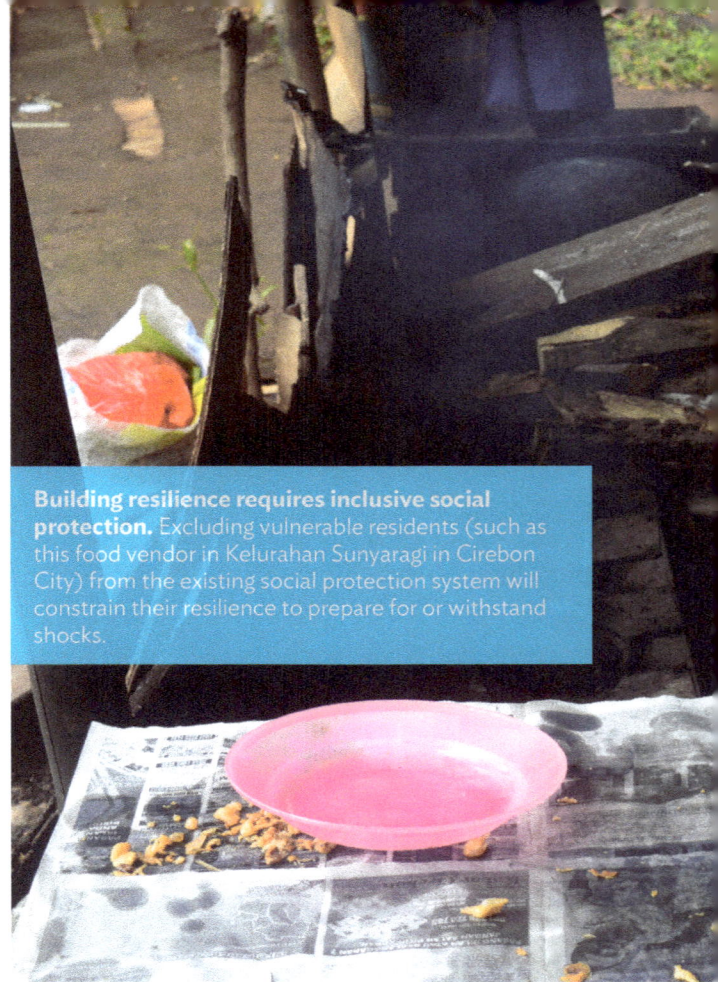

Building resilience requires inclusive social protection. Excluding vulnerable residents (such as this food vendor in Kelurahan Sunyaragi in Cirebon City) from the existing social protection system will constrain their resilience to prepare for or withstand shocks.

costs associated with education, absorbing a similar level of expenditure to PKH. Cash transfers are also provided to older persons (through Asistensi Sosial Lanjut Usia Terlantar, or ASLUT) and people with disabilities (through Asistensi Sosial Penyandang Disabilitas Berat, or ASPDB). *Zakat* (alms-giving) has an important role in Indonesian society to address the incidence, depth, and severity of poverty.[33] The national public health insurance scheme, Programme Jaminan Kesehatan Nasional (JKN), is funded predominantly by member contributions and currently reaches 200 million people but fully subsidizes the contributions for the poorest 40% of the population known as Penerima Bayaran Iuran (PBI) beneficiaries (see section 3.2). Furthermore, approximately 15% of the working-age population that are primarily from the formal sector (referred to as wage recipients) is covered by employment insurance, such as work injury compensation, old age savings with disability benefit, old age pension,

---

[32] Carbohydrates: rice, corn kernels and sago; Animal protein: eggs, beef, chicken and fresh fish; Vegetable protein: beans, including tempeh and tofu; Sources of vitamins and minerals: vegetables and fruits.

[33] All Muslims who are eligible to donate are obliged to share 2.5% of their accumulated income or wealth for the benefit of the poor and the needy.

has limited features to strengthen climate resilience for the urban poor. At present, covariate shocks—those which affect an entire community or areas, such as floods—are not addressed through the social protection system. However, the ongoing innovative responses to COVID-19 through reallocating a portion of their village funds to provide unconditional cash transfers and cash-for-work programs[34] to 12.3 million beneficiaries is a promising pathway that can equally happen in responding to other covariate shocks including the climate and disaster risks.[35]

Scaling up social protection for the urban poor would require addressing multiple barriers in building urban poor resilience.

First, in terms of coverage, social protection for many urban households is limited, hampering their capacity to be resilient in the face of shocks. Excluding vulnerable urban residents from most of the existing social protection system will constrain their resilience to prepare for or withstand shocks. For example, contributory social insurance schemes cover many affluent households in the formal sector, and the government provides substantial noncontributory support to a large proportion of poor and vulnerable households across the country. However, many of the "missing middle"—those living on vulnerable incomes and not benefiting from any form of social protection aside from health insurance—are in urban areas. Low urban coverage is therefore driven in part by social assistance programs focusing predominantly on income poverty to the exclusion of vulnerability and multidimensional poverty considerations. If such considerations were taken into account, the eligibility for social protection in urban areas would be much higher. For instance, urban multidimensional poverty in Indonesia was 18.5%

and survivors' benefit. With these predictable and timely cash transfers, the adaptive capacity of the households increases to tackle the underlying vulnerability to various risks, including climate and disaster risk.

Climate change response is not mainstreamed in social protection programs. Various line ministries are responsible for implementation of social protection programs, particularly the Ministry of Social Affairs, the Ministry of Education and Culture, the Ministry of Religious Affairs, and the Ministry of Health with oversight function by the Coordinating Ministry for Human Development and Cultural Affairs and the National Development Planning Agency (BAPPENAS). However, climate and disaster risk considerations are not made explicit in the design objectives and delivery features of urban poor programs, nor within the broader objectives of social protection at large. For example, neither geographical nor household targeting focuses explicitly on criteria related to climate and disaster risk in urban areas. The current design of social protection in Indonesia therefore

---

34   Cash has been provided to residents affected by the crisis but not recipients of any other social assistance programs, with beneficiary selection determined through community consultation processes.

35   Ministry of Village, Development of Disadvantaged Regions and Transmigration (Kemendesa). BLT Rp600.000/Bulan, Begini Cara Pemerintah Data Penerimanya (in Indonesian).

in 2014, even though monetary poverty was much lower at 8.4%.[36] The lack of frequency of updating, validating, and verifying household rankings in the DTKS also limits its utilization for horizontal expansion or creation of new programs, as the DTKS is not able to identify populations that are temporarily poor and/or those who are potentially vulnerable to future shocks (particularly rapid onset). However, there have been encouraging developments as initial attempts are being made by the Data and Information Center (PUSDATIN) in the Ministry of Social Affairs to integrate area-based risk information into the DTKS.

Second, in terms of adequacy, the generosity of the transfer level of the social assistance is unlikely to be adequate to address the needs of urban households, thus limiting their resilience to prepare for and withstand shocks. Evidence shows that routine social assistance in Indonesia has had positive impacts on human capital and poverty reduction,[37] although may not necessarily representative the same impact in urban areas due to the higher cost of living, coupled with the low beneficiary coverage in urban areas. International evidence on urban social protection illustrates the importance of adapting social assistance to urban settings. This includes specifically assessing the costs and constraints faced by poor urban households, the role of human capital in strengthening urban resilience, and the tailoring of support and eligibility accordingly.[38] Furthermore, ensuring the availability of contingency funding for social assistance programs is crucial to enable the social protection system to respond accordingly and to allow expansion of transfer levels or caseloads during an emergency to accommodate a vertical or horizontal expansion.

Third, in terms of comprehensiveness, vulnerable households in Indonesia's urban areas face multifaceted constraints, and many of these needs are not met by social protection. As noted earlier, structural inequalities such as gender norms, social rules, class, and uneven power relations all intersect and contribute to the multidimensional vulnerability of the urban poor, large numbers of whom have also migrated from rural areas. The disadvantages faced by women relative to men are compounded over the course of the life cycle (footnote 4), with households headed by women often highly vulnerable and facing discrimination in the labor market in terms of both employment opportunities and wages. While recognizing the constraints on the extent to which social protection on its own can achieve longer-term and second-order impacts related to social or economic outcomes,[39] urban residents face unmet needs. Notwithstanding the existing access for many to health insurance, they will continue to face challenges related to issues such as housing, childcare, or gender-based violence. The low coverage of urban beneficiaries by social assistance measures means there are limited opportunities for supporting the resilience of the urban poor including climate and disaster-related shocks and stresses.

Fourth, in terms of delivery systems, the social protection system is poorly equipped to cope with high levels of mobility. While many attributes of delivery systems for social protection in Indonesia are encouraging, an existing constraint relates to the mobility of individuals, households, and populations, within cities and between cities, towns, and rural areas. Programs like PKH address this on paper; when a household deemed eligible for PKH moves between rural and urban areas,

36   Oxford Poverty and Human Development Initiative. 2015. Calculation: Multidimensional Poverty Index Indonesia, 2012–2014. Executive Summary.
37   For example, beneficiaries of PKH have experienced reduced stunting (by 9–11 percentage points), increased primary school enrollment (by 4 percentage points), increased secondary school enrollment (by 8 percentage points), and increased consumption and healthy behaviors (footnote 32).
38   J. Behrman, J. Gallardo-García, S. Parker, P. Todd, and V. Vélez-Grajales. 2012. Are Conditional Cash Transfers Effective in Urban Areas? Evidence from Mexico. Education Economics. 20 (3). pp. 233–259.

39   K. Roelen, S. Devereux, A-G. Abdulai, B. Martorano, T. Palermo, and L.P. Ragno. 2017. How to Make "Cash Plus" Work: Linking Cash Transfers to Services and Sectors. Innocenti Working Papers No. 2017-10. Florence, Italy.

their PKH eligibility moves with them in the immediate term. It is less clear, however, at which point they are assessed differently based on their new location. Currently, the Ministry of Social Affairs is working on adapting PKH to ensure some populations in remote, underserved areas do not need to fill all the conditionalities associated to receive benefits. The importance of the portability feature of the social protection system becomes critical in the context of climate-induced migration. Moreover, the solid progress in strengthening Indonesia's delivery systems for routine social protection will be of limited assistance due to the low coverage of urban residents through existing schemes.

Fifth, in terms of governance and coordination, the capacity of government officials to enhance urban resilience and address the social protection needs of urban households may be constrained. Building resilience for the urban poor requires governance and coordination structures that are coherent between social protection, climate change adaptation, and disaster risk management programs. Increased coordination will be required between national and subnational governments due to less familiarity of the central-level staff with the unique challenges on the ground for best way forward in building urban resilience. Delivering adaptive social protection also requires coordination of different ministries involved in social protection (including the Ministry of Social Affairs) with the national agencies mandated with climate change adaptation and disaster risk management—the Ministry of Environment and Forestry and Badan Nasional Penanggulangan Bencana (BNPB), respectively.

Sixth, enhancing the country's social protection system to address the current and future vulnerabilities of the urban poor will be challenging due to inadequate systems and low coverage. The social assistance system is not yet equipped with the operational mechanisms to "flex" in response to shocks to help protect urban poor households in their consumption and access

to services before, during, and after climate and disaster-related shocks and stresses. Potential options include vertical expansion (increased transfer levels) for existing beneficiaries, and expansion of caseloads through horizontal expansion (providing transfers to additional beneficiaries on a temporary basis), or creation of new programs in affected areas. However, the low coverage of both social assistance and social insurance in urban areas would hinder the reach of any vertical expansion in response to a shock.

Scaling up initiatives that strengthen social protection resilience to become 'adaptive' and 'shock-responsive' will require a range of interventions:

- **Climate considerations should be explicitly incorporated into urban social protection initiatives in Indonesia.** This involves considering the extent to which social protection can help urban residents adapt to climate shocks (e.g., strengthen their capacity to withstand extreme shocks without external financial assistance) and mitigate the risks in the face of changing climates and weather patterns (e.g., improve the capacity of urban beneficiaries to provide food and nutrition for their families).[40] Urban social protection measures in Indonesia can capitalize on the growing momentum to "build forward sustainably" in the wake of COVID-19. By viewing social protection as an important adaptation strategy, the opportunity for accessing climate finance for such investments will also potentially increase.

- **Expand urban coverage of routine social protection to build resilience to shocks that allows to adapt and expand horizontally in the event of a shock.** Successful adaptive social protection is underpinned by accurate, relevant, and timely data, including with regard

40   J. Lind, K. Roelen, and R. Sabates-Wheeler. 2020. *Social Protection and Building Back Better*. Positioning Paper. Brighton: Institute of Development Studies.

to early warning systems and recognizing emerging needs. By including a broad base of households in the DTKS, the social protection system becomes equipped to rapidly identify (and support) a larger number of households than the existing pool of beneficiaries in the event of a shock. Determining which urban beneficiaries to include should be informed by integrating poverty and vulnerability data with disaster risk assessments. This will enable the DTKS to incorporate a spatial understanding of household vulnerability to seasonal or sudden onset shocks and facilitate adaptive social protection programming through the integration of social protection with disaster risk management strategies (footnote 4). The integration of good-quality, dynamic, and accessible data on natural hazards, exposure, and vulnerability can help to understand more accurately the degree to which current social protection programs are helping ameliorate risk as well as the gaps that need to be filled through change in program design and/or through new initiatives. This will involve analysis of data systems (e.g., DTKS and SIDIK, an online vulnerability analysis system used to calculate an area's Vulnerability Index, see section 4.2) to explore the degree to which such systems are fit for collecting and verifying data in urban areas on poverty and climate and disaster risk.[41]

- **Improve the contribution of social protection to urban resilience by designing transfer levels.** The regular transfers should be designed to help households to both minimize the likely harmful effects of climate and disaster risk through *ex ante* actions and expedite efficient response and recovery in the aftermath of an event through *ex post* measures.[42] This includes

delivering the correct amount of social transfers to beneficiaries in a regular and predictable manner. With urban areas particularly susceptible to food and fuel price changes, beneficiary households will remain poor or vulnerable if the level of transfers received is inadequate. It is also crucial to ensure transfer levels are designed to meet individual and household needs (e.g., household size and structure, age, gender, and disability-related needs) and to factor in the real value of transfers by reflecting the inflationary pressures and adjustments to restore purchasing power. Indonesia has made strong progress in enhancing its operational and payment systems for routine social assistance, and these efforts should be maintained and strengthened.

- **Strengthen *ex ante* resilience by establishing links between urban social protection beneficiaries and other services.** Linking beneficiaries with climate services and programs on livelihoods, building skills, financial inclusion, and social empowerment (especially of women) can help to strengthen livelihoods of poor and vulnerable households in the face of climate risks and increase their capacity to cope with shocks. Labor-intensive market programs can directly support implementation of resilience measures such as soil conservation, water conservation, and agroforestry, while providing income earning opportunities for the urban poor during lean periods and in the aftermath of large-scale disasters. Establishing the agreed vision *ex ante* across government, effective coordination mechanisms, and protocols will be required for the design and implementation of emergency assistance and shock-responsive social assistance. However, establishing linkages is clearly a complex and expansive agenda that presents many challenges, including fiscal constraints as well

---

[41] Undertaking such action will require close collaboration with the Ministry of Environment and Forestry and BNPB. It will also require significant financial resources, which can potentially be supported by international climate finance, recognizing the transformational impact such actions would have in the future.

[42] ADB. 2018. *Strengthening Resilience through Social Protection Programs* (Guidance Note). Manila.

as the need for buy-in and commitment from other sectors.

- **Enhance financing structure for adaptive social protection.** Having pre-agreed funding sources in place at all levels of government and agreeing on disbursement channels for the fund transfers to flow effectively when a shock happens and reach beneficiaries quickly is of utmost importance to strengthen the resilience of the urban poor beneficiaries. The mix of instruments might include contingency budgets, multiyear national and local disaster funds, contingent credit, and risk transfer instruments such as insurance. It may also be necessary to develop dedicated sources of finance for strengthened investment (including domestic revenue generation) while ensuring that current financing is maintained in the face of intensified competition for limited funds. Therefore it will be crucial to explicitly explore the link between shock-responsive social protection programs and Disaster Risk Financing and Insurance instruments, including forecast-based financing that allows the use of weather and climate information to anticipate possible impacts in risk-prone areas and mobilize resources before an event occurs. Based on lessons from the COVID-19 pandemic, financial options should also be explored in the context of fiscal balance transfer such as the Kelurahan Fund.

- **Strengthen coordination and raise awareness on urban poor resilience.** The good understanding of the nexus of urban poverty and climate and disaster resilience, and how social protection programs can contribute to improve the urban poor resilience at national, provincial, district, and local levels become the critical success factor for strengthening the urban poor resilience at the household levels.

By collaborating with the local actors relevant to urban social protection such as the CSOs, private sector actors, and urban communities themselves can help to set the priorities and design of urban programs; outreaching communication messages; contributing to advocacy and accountability efforts; and supporting processes related to targeting, identification, payments[43] and developing tailored insurance and financial products for poor and vulnerable groups, employment programs, and climate service delivery.[44] Increased awareness of the social workers (facilitators) on climate and disaster risk is crucial, especially in the context of the four priority sectors identified in PBI 2020-2045 and including the spatial and temporal characteristics of climate risks. Links should be explored with the Ministry of Social Affairs TAGANA program, which focuses on building capacity of village-level volunteers on disaster preparedness and response and the Kampung Siance Bencana (Disaster Preparedness Village) Program. Where available, partnerships should be strengthened for preparedness measures with Kelompok Siaga Bencana (KSB)—community-based disaster preparedness groups established by BNPB implemented Pengembangan Desa/Kelurahan Tangguh Bencana – DESTANA/KATANA (Disaster Resilient Village/Neighborhood) program and trained to be able to identify hazards, develop contingency plans, and implement disaster.

43 For more information on localization, see C. Cabot Venton et al. 2020. Embedding Localization in the Response to COVID-19. Social Protection Approaches to COVID-19 - Expert Advice Helpline, SPACE; FCDO and GIZ.

44 M. Aleksandrova. 2019. Principles and Considerations for Mainstreaming Climate Change Risk into National Social Protection Frameworks in Developing Countries. *Climate and Development*. 12 (6). pp. 511–520.

Resilience through Sustainable Livelihoods

Climate risk threatens the livelihoods of the urban poor. Urban poor workers are often engaged in the informal economy with an unstable income that makes them vulnerable to shocks including climate-related shocks. Moreover, they may "not be poor enough" to qualify for social assistance or "not formal enough" to qualify for social insurance, thereby leading to a segment of the population being largely underserved by social protection (footnote 4). Studies of street vendors in Yogyakarta demonstrate that their financial position is precarious regardless of climate change, so that even a mild disturbance can lead to the disruption of their livelihood.[45] With climate change, rapid onset hazards will increase in the future. Moreover, climate change can also impact the natural capital on which many urban and peri-urban livelihoods are based. For instance, a large number of the urban poor in the coastal areas are engaged in fishing. Climate change is, however, starting to have a negative impact on this as water temperatures are rising, leading to inhospitable living and breeding conditions for fish. Estimates suggest that climate change could lead to around a decrease of 13% (RCP2.6) to 29% (RCP8.5) in total fisheries catch potential in Indonesian waters by 2050, depending on the emissions scenario.[46] Similarly, peri-urban farming is and will continue to be negatively impacted by rising temperatures; destruction of the topsoil by extreme rainfall events; and increased pathogens, insect attacks, and parasites. The reduction in crop yields in rural areas due to change in climate would affect food prices and impact consumption patterns of urban poor households. Climate change also has a deleterious impact on infrastructure and the built environment without which urban livelihoods are not possible. Rapid onset hazards can destroy public transport infrastructure, factories, workshops, stalls, and shops upon which the urban poor depend for their livelihood. Thus, it is important to invest in resilient livelihoods for the urban poor in Indonesia, and to also ensure that initiatives that encourage livelihood shifts, entrepreneurship, or business development do not inadvertently increase vulnerability by pushing the urban poor toward livelihoods options that could make them more vulnerable to the impacts of disasters and climate change.

A combination of measures is critical to strengthen climate resilience of the urban poor. Such a combination of measures for livelihood resilience includes savings and safety nets; income stability and diversity; education, skills, and mindset; and social networks and mobility.[47] Savings and safety nets can enable households to cover income needs during lean periods, have funds to adopt coping mechanisms to deal with shocks and stresses, and most importantly invest in resilience measures. Having a stable income enables a household to provide for their living needs and to build their savings and safety nets, and income diversity reduces the reliance of the household on one income source to meet their daily needs. The education and skills of each person in the household heavily dictates the type of livelihood activities they can perform, as well as the choices they make in preparing their household in advance to respond to different types of risks. Having household members that are socially mobile—able to move between different classes and networks of people—and have a large social network is advantageous for any household for increasing the exposure to new ideas, opening

---

45   A.G. Brata. 2010. Vulnerability of Urban Informal Sector: Street Vendors in Yogyakarta, Indonesia. *Theoretical and Empirical Researches in Urban Management*. 5 (5).

46   M. Barange, T. Bahri, M. Beveridge, K. Cochrane, S. Funge-Smith, and F. Poulain. 2018. Impacts of Climate Change on Fisheries and Aquaculture: Synthesis of Current Knowledge, Adaptation and Mitigation Options. Food and Agriculture Organization of the United Nations (FAO) Technical Paper No. 627.

47   ADB. 2020. *Advancing Inclusive and Resilient Urban Development Targeted at the Urban Poor*. Consultant's report. Manila (TA 9513-REG)

new opportunities, and potentially generating new income sources (footnote 47).

Indonesia has a rich constellation of policies and programs focused on ensuring strong and stable livelihoods. The RPJMN 2020–2024 provides a strong policy impetus for livelihood development in the context of poverty alleviation, where the government commits to addressing the poverty and strengthening livelihoods macro and micro policy actions through increasing productivity, seeking and creating employment, and supporting economic development and social protection. Indonesia has been implementing a range of programs across different categories to support the livelihoods of the urban poor.

First, programs focused on vocational training and skills development. One example is Balai Latihan Kerja or vocational training centers to provide skills training to the urban poor with a view to enhancing their employment prospects. The Kartu Pra Kerja (Pre-Employment Card Program) digital platform allows those looking for employment to find the most suitable training opportunity, make connections with potential employers, and access financial support for the training and unemployment benefits.

Second, labor-intensive livelihood programs whose main purpose is providing a basic income in off-seasons to the poor. A good example of this is Padat Karya Tunai (PKT), which is being linked to a range of development programs such as the Acceleration Program for Irrigation Improvement, Construction of Artificial Aquifers for Rainwater Savings, and the City without Slums (KOTAKU).

Third, initiatives that provide credit and other inputs to enable entrepreneurship and self-employment. Peningkatan Penghidupan Masyarakat Berbasis Komunitas was implemented from 2012 to 2014 to provide micro loans to businesses run by low-income communities. This was primarily done through self-help groups to ensure that finances are invested in productive livelihood opportunities

that also deliver social and environment benefits. Of the self-help groups, 90% established under this program have secured funding and invested this in strengthening the livelihoods of the urban poor.

Fourth, programs that aim to strengthen climate resilience while improving livelihoods. A good example of this is the Kampung Iklim Program (ProKlim) that operates across rural and urban areas. Though not strictly a livelihood program, it has a thrust to ensure that livelihoods can withstand the impacts of climate change. It seeks out and awards local-level innovations aimed at enhancing the resilience for life and livelihood changes. This has included novel water resource management systems, urban agriculture schemes, composting, and flood early warning systems that strengthen livelihoods while also increasing resilience. Taken together, the range of programs can be seen as making an important contribution to the underlying assets and livelihoods of the urban poor that can help this group become more resilient to shocks and stresses.

The informal nature of livelihood strategies adopted by the urban poor is a hurdle to the provision of resilience support. First, the urban poor in Indonesia are frequently informal workers who are not linked to formal banking systems and are not registered on government databases. Being beyond the purview of formal systems means that enrolling them in structured and systematic livelihood programs is difficult. This issue will only increase with climate change, with a substantial proportion of this group migrating in and out of cities to take advantage of seasonal employment opportunities in villages and urban areas and considered to be temporary workers. Their livelihood strategies are often ad hoc and fragile, and this in turn reduces their capacity to adapt to shocks and stresses.

Second, gaps in data make the delivery of initiatives to strengthen livelihoods difficult. The government has made substantial attempts to upgrade the level and quality of data being gathered on

Informal livelihood. A woman sells cooked food at Glodok market, West Jakarta.

the urban poor in order to design and deliver appropriate poverty alleviation and livelihood programming. For instance, the National Team for the Acceleration of Poverty Reduction (TNP2K) aggregated poverty data to enable targeting and facilitated coordination among ministries for the delivery of appropriate assistance. Despite such attempts, data tend to be static and inaccurate and exclude large numbers of those who need assistance. Even as poverty data remain scant and incomplete, the lack of data on the risk that the urban poor face adds another layer of challenges to the delivery livelihood-strengthening initiatives for enhancing resilience. While the government is

attempting to overcome some of these challenges through the development of the integrated databases (e.g., DTKS) for social welfare-related data, the impact of this is yet to be seen.

Third, a large percentage of the urban poor are employed in micro, small, and medium-sized enterprises (MSMEs). Often located in communities, these enterprises share similar types of hazards with the wider community. In addition, they are also affected by shocks and stresses in other areas due to their supply chain and distribution networks. The enterprises typically have low levels of resilience to deal recent COVID-19 crisis. For example, the arrival of COVID-19 almost immediately closed or severely impacted the operations of enterprises as reported by 81% of survey respondents in 2020.[49] Thus, during the COVID-19 recovery period, creating a bridging loan fund will be important so that the "unbankable" enterprises can access small business capital support.

Fourth, microfinance is recognized as one strategy to provide support for the urban poor in developing informal microenterprises that can provide household income and contribute to income diversification (footnote 47). However, microfinance institutions do not necessarily have resilience strategies in place to support their clients in times of shock. For example, microfinance institutions may not have timely access to liquidity to support their clients after a disaster.

Scaling up initiatives that strengthen livelihood resilience will require a range of interventions:

- **Introduce targeted policy shifts in select areas to realize the full potential of strengthening resilience.** Carefully targeted shifts in specific policy areas can ensure the livelihood resilience of the urban poor. First, identifying and including those within the informal economy in livelihood programs need to be emphasized and their resilience strengthened through access to finance, skills, and information. This should also include a focus on the migrant population to deal with seasonal climate risk or long-term impacts on their settlements and livelihoods. Second, attempts should be made to upgrade the data environment for the design and delivery of livelihood programs to better understand their direct and indirect linkages with long-term climate risk, especially in priority sectors of PBI 2020–2045, such as agriculture, water, and marine and coastal.

with shocks, due to various factors such as low understanding of hazards, limited capacity for business continuity management, and limited access to disaster risk financing instruments.[48] A 2015 survey revealed that the coping mechanisms employed by the MSMEs are largely self-reliant and dependent on close connections and support from family and friends. Such mechanisms could be less effective during large-scale events that may affect the entire community. The limited resilience of enterprises was exposed in the

---

48   Asian Disaster Preparedness Center. 2016. *Strengthening Disaster and Climate Resilience of Small and Medium Enterprises in Asia: Indonesia.*

49   United Nations Industrial Development Organization. 2020. Summary of COVID-19 Impact Assessment on SME in Indonesia.

This can be done by developing better protocols for different ministries delivering programs to share information and by drawing on databases from other sectors (e.g., SIDIK and InaRISK) that might contain information relevant to the development of such programs. Third, a major thrust on innovation, including innovative financial products that can strengthen livelihood resilience, is needed within livelihood programs. Current programs do not provide the right impetus for accelerating entrepreneurial experimentation for the development new and more robust livelihood strategies. This is particularly important in the context of climate change where novel solutions are needed to enhance resilience. Last, a focus on strengthening resilience of MSMEs is critical. Future updates of climate change adaptation plans should look at implications of climate risk on rural and urban livelihoods in Indonesia.

- **Mainstream climate risk considerations in the design of livelihood programs.** Given the close link between livelihoods and climate risk, livelihood-strengthening programs may require a major shift in strategies and institutions. This will require a robust understanding of the range of plausible impacts of current and future climate risk on livelihood-related sectors and introduction of new strategies, processes, and protocols to deal with risk. For example, the Padat Karya Tunai (PKT) program can better integrate long-term climate risk information so that the irrigation infrastructure or artificial aquifers being delivered as part of this are appropriate to changes in rainfall patterns that climate change is likely to induce; and the Pemberdayaan Ekonomi Masyarakat Pesisir or Coastal Community Economic Empowerment initiative that aims at developing alternative livelihoods for poor coastal communities can ensure that these alternative options are less prone to climate change or disaster impacts, thereby facilitating transformational adaptation.

- **Strengthen training and skill development programs to cater to changing market needs and thereby strengthen resilience.** Expanding access to market-relevant training and skill development is an important way of increasing the potential for a household to stabilize or diversify their income sources, and thereby be resilient to shocks and stresses. For example, given the ongoing innovations in digital technology and considering the impacts of COVID-19, digital literacy and skills required for e-commerce, for example, are one area to prioritize for the urban poor (footnote 47). Such skills will help them cope with future shocks, including climate-related shocks. In the context of changing climate risk, it is important to ensure that people who are forced to migrate to deal with climate stresses have access to new skills that help them find economic opportunities in urban areas.

- **Design livelihood programs to respond to the local context of changing risk.** Localization would ensure that livelihood programs are meeting the specific needs of vulnerable communities and also that their livelihoods are more resilient. This can be done in a number of ways, for example through the Kelurahan Fund (see section 4.3) at the neighborhood level. This is primarily employed for the development of local infrastructure, but there is growing realization of the need for this finance to also support the strengthening of livelihoods for vulnerable communities in urban areas. The analogous funds in rural areas (i.e., the Village Fund) has been successfully using fund transfers for supporting livelihood development and provides a valuable precedent for urban areas. Another suggestion for resilient livelihoods is supporting the development of clusters of individuals and enterprises pursuing similar strategies for securing livelihoods. Providing incentives for artisans, craft workers, and cottage industries in

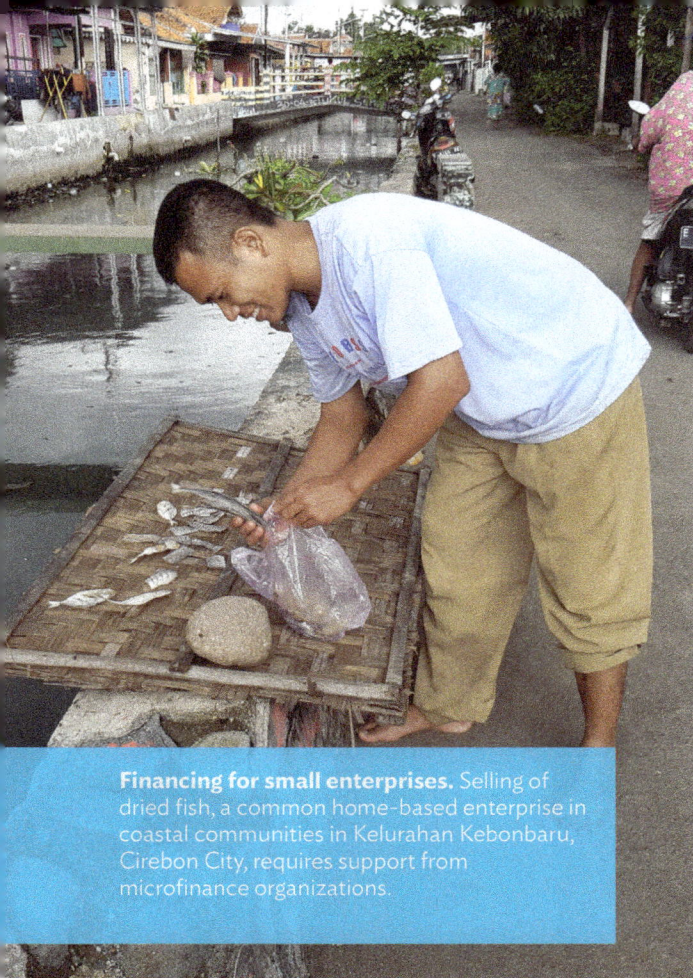

Financing for small enterprises. Selling of dried fish, a common home-based enterprise in coastal communities in Kelurahan Kebonbaru, Cirebon City, requires support from microfinance organizations.

similar businesses to be located in similar areas allows them to network, develop cooperative marketing strategies, exchange knowledge, and demand better prices from intermediaries and raw material providers. This clustering also enables the authorities to more effectively provide better tailored support for livelihood strengthening in the form of capacity-building, insurance, or small loans. Crucially, this also enables the development of adaptation and resilience strategies that are specifically designed for each cluster. Undertaking these measures that are rooted locally and employ decentralized governance approaches will also ensure that a number of those considered "informal" and invisible in formal government databases can be identified and included by local actors managing these schemes.

- **Strengthen resilience of micro, small, and medium-sized enterprises.** The MSMEs are known to be a major employer of the urban poor.

Thus, it is critical to have dedicated initiatives to strengthen the resilience of these enterprises, including a range of measures to increase awareness about natural hazards, such as their changing patterns and implications on supply chain; enhance participation in community disaster preparedness activities; build capacity for business continuity planning; and improve access to disaster insurance. Such measures can help MSMEs improve their coping capacity and incrementally adapt to climate change. Longer-term strategies may also be needed to adapt to changes in climate, especially for the enterprises closely associated to the four key sectors of PBI 2020-2045, thereby facilitating transformational adaptation. Strengthening resilience of the MSMEs will require close collaboration with the Ministry of Cooperatives and SMEs, and engagement with private sector organizations, such as the Asosiasi Pengusaha Indonesia – APINDO (Employers' Association of Indonesia) and Kamar Dagang dan Industri Indonesia – KADIN (Indonesian Chamber of Commerce and Industry).

- **Introduce disaster-resilient microfinance.** Microfinance organizations offer a portfolio of financial products to support the livelihood of the urban poor. They can establish a disaster contingency fund that affected members can avail of to repair their houses damaged by a natural hazard or to restore livelihoods or productive assets. As part of their assistance, they can provide training on resilient livelihood practices, financial literacy, and basic business skills, and raise awareness on effects of climate and disasters on livelihood. It is important that microfinance organizations have access to concessional finance to support their urban poor clients. As the microfinance industry continues to expand, greater support should be extended to microfinance organizations that contribute to building resilience of the urban poor.

Resilience through Effective Public Health System

Future climate will have large implications on the health of the urban poor. Climate change is likely to affect the health of the urban poor negatively in several ways. First, high exposure to flooding affects health. Apart from causing death from drowning, floodwaters can pollute drinking water sources, and stagnant floodwaters bring the threat of disease and amplify the distribution of disease vectors. Over the long term, floods may lead to population displacement, which can lead to other associated health impacts.[50] Second, shifts in climate variables are likely to improve the breeding conditions for a number of infectious diseases including malaria and dengue. Estimates suggest that dengue fever events will be very high until 2045 in various cities, such as Pekanbaru, Palembang, Banjarbaru, Banjarmasin, Samarinda, Tarakan, Kolaka, Ambon, Semarang, Bali, and Kupang.[51] Under both high and low emission scenarios, about 308 million people are projected to be at risk of malaria by 2070, if attempts to control the disease are not expanded and strengthened (footnote 50). Third, the urban poor are particularly prone to the impacts of extreme heat as their livelihood patterns increase their exposure, and they are unable to afford artificial cooling. Heat-related deaths in Indonesia, especially among the elderly, could increase by more than 50 times by 2080 (under a high emissions scenario) (footnote 50). Fourth, there are a whole range of potential indirect impacts of climate change on health, such as those arising from a lack of adequate nutrition due to food insecurity. All four dimensions of food security—food availability, food accessibility, food utilization, and food system stability—are prone to climate change. Furthermore, escalating food prices arising from the impact of climate change on agriculture is a threat for the urban poor.

The poor in Indonesia are particularly vulnerable to an increase in food prices; theoretical modeling shows that a 100% increase in food prices would increase the number of Indonesians living in extreme poverty by more than 25%.[52]

An effective public health system is crucial to build the resilience of the urban poor and to reduce their costs of health care and inability to pursue livelihoods. An effective public health system with facilities and human resources allows the urban poor to access facilities with promotive and preventive functions, which would help reduce exposure to disease, and with curative and rehabilitative functions to respond and recover. Achieving an effective public health system would require quality health facilities and infrastructure that are capable of facing the impacts of extreme weather events, as well as integrated health systems capable of accommodating spikes in demand due to climate-induced extreme events and dealing with shifting disease patterns through improved alert systems, type, quantity, and quality of health human resources, pharmacy and medical devices, information systems, research and development, and financing. Moreover, since many of the social and environmental determinants of health lie in non-health-related sectors such as safe drinking water, sanitation facilities, sufficient availability of food, and secure shelter, the effectiveness of a public health system is also a function of non-health sectors. The importance of an effective public health system has been put to the test in the recent COVID-19 pandemic.

---

[50] World Health Organization (WHO) and United Nations Framework Convention on Climate Change. 2016. *Health and Climate Change: Country Profile 2015: Indonesia*. Geneva: WHO.

[51] BAPPENAS. 2020. *National Action Plan for Climate Change Adaptation (RAN-API)*. PowerPoint presentation. 26 February.

[52] S. Hallegatte, M. Bangalore, L. Bonzanigo, M. Fay, T. Kane, U. Narloch, J. Rozenberg, D. Treguer, and A. Vogt-Schilb. 2016. Shock Waves: Managing the Impacts of Climate Change on Poverty. *Climate Change and Development Series*. Washington, DC: World Bank. p. 58.

Indonesia's public health system and wider policies provide a good foundation for building resilience of the urban poor. The pursuit of universal health coverage marks a significant expansion of Indonesian health and social policy from targeting the upper and lower ends of the income spectrum to a more inclusive approach.[53] The national health insurance program, Jaminan Kesehatan Nasional (JKN), is a hybrid system as it combines assistance (premium payment for poor households is subsidized) and insurance (richer households pay into the program) initiated in January 2014. JKN is executed by a social security organizing body, the Badan Penyelenggara Jaminan Sosial Kesehatan (BPJS-Kesehatan).[54] As of March 2020, there were 222,386,830 JKN participants (85% of the Indonesian population).[55] In the RPJMN 2020–2024, JKN is targeted to reach 98% of the population by 2024.[56] There are important examples of how, at city level, JKN has been adapted to respond to the needs of vulnerable groups. In Yogyakarta, for example, the government has taken measures to address this by providing financial support to persons with disability and those who do not have health insurance. This demonstrates the potential of JKN to support the urban poor in dealing with climate risk. At a wider policy level, PBI 2020-2045 has identified health as one of the strategic priorities for climate change adaptation and recommended a set of delivery strategies, including expansion of health infrastructure on the basis of climate risk information, improvement in early warning systems, education and awareness on climate risk and health, and development of new standards, laws, and regulations for reducing climate-induced diseases. The Ministry of Health has established an ad hoc committee to respond to climate change, including a technical team charged with examining the impact of climate on the health sector and devising adaptation actions. Furthermore, the ministry has made a concerted effort to increase the surveillance of diseases that are influenced by a changing climate such as diarrhea, pneumonia, malaria, influenza-like illness, and dengue—all of which have significant impacts on the poor living in urban areas.[57]

It is imperative to add a national plan for adaptation to climate change in health (RAN APIK), which is also equipped with an application system for mapping the vulnerability of areas. This serves as a reference for the contribution of the health sector to climate change resilience.

Links between health and other sectors are also recognized for building resilience. These include food security, improved water supply and sanitation, and health and climate risk. Adequate nutrition for the urban poor depends on the availability of affordable and nutritious food. As climate change is likely to affect both the production (and price) of food, and potentially the quality of this food (e.g., through higher temperatures increasing spoilage), strengthening urban food systems is an important element of building resilience of the urban poor.[58] PBI 2020–2045 recognizes the link between food security and climate impacts and Law No. 18/2012 Governing Food Security in Indonesia ensures that food is available and affordable to meet the demands of the country's population. This law provides a powerful mandate to various government agencies to implement a range of plans and programs for enhancing food security—although this has not always included an explicit focus on the urban poor. PBI 2020–2045 promotes Climate Smart Agriculture and identified efficient irrigation and

53   M. Sumarto and A. Kaasch. 2018. New Directions in Social Policy: Evidence from the Indonesian Health Insurance Programme. *UNRISD Working Paper* 2018–9.
54   Haryanto, B. 2020. *Urban Health, Climate Risk and Resilience.* Background paper for the Asian Development Bank.
55   Social Security Administrator for Health (BPJS Kesehatan)
56   BAPPENAS. Government Development Plan and Work Plan Portal. *The National Medium-Term Development Plan for 2020–2024.*

57   B. Haryanto. 2018. Indonesia Dengue Fever: Status, Vulnerability, and Challenges. In A.J. Rodriguez-Morales, ed. *Current Topics in Tropical Emerging Diseases and Travel Medicine.* IntechOpen.
58   C. Tacoli. 2019. The Urbanization of Food Insecurity and Malnutrition. *Environment and Urbanization.* 31 (2). pp. 371–374.

Linking health with other sectors builds resilience. Raising community awareness on the link between contaminated water and the spread of certain diseases can help improve health and resilience of the urban poor (photo by RISE Program).

flood control among the priority climates resilience actions in the agriculture sector.

The COVID-19 pandemic exposed the weakness of Indonesia's public health system. The country has one of the lowest ratios of health workers to the population in Asia at 4.3 medical doctors and 24.1 nursing and midwifery personnel for every 10,000 persons. This is well short of the current Sustainable Development Goal threshold of 44.5 health workers per 10,000 population.[59] The enormous COVID-19 workload overwhelmed Indonesia's health system and forced the government to rely on military and security agencies for contact tracing, delivery of medical equipment

aids, disinfection, and coronavirus education.[60] High levels of civic and social participation in Indonesia also highlighted the importance of social responses to support crisis management and recovery and to complement medical efforts. Crowdfunding campaigns supported informal sector workers and provided personal protective equipment (PPE) for health-care workers. Thousands of medical students volunteered for deployment as COVID-19 rapid response teams. Academic institutions led research and development into PPE, COVID-19 rapid testing instruments, and treatments. Telemedicine apps also rose in popularity due to efforts of start-ups in the digital sector, providing COVID-19 consultation services, booking appointments

---

59   World Health Organization. 2020. World Health Statistics 2020: *Monitoring Health for the SDGs, Sustainable Development Goals.* Geneva.

60   T. Chairil. 2020. Indonesia's Intelligence Service is Coming Out to Counter COVID-19. *The Diplomat.* 19 June.

for COVID-19 rapid tests, and purchasing and delivering prescription medicine.[61] The national government and Chamber of Commerce (Kadin) also started implementing Vaksinati Gotong Royong in May 2021 to accelerate the coverage of COVID-19 vaccinations by allowing companies to arrange the vaccination of their employees and dependents.[62] Several companies made their network of cold-storage units available to accommodate vaccine inventories while some opened their facilities to become vaccination sites.[63] These partnerships among communities, local governments, health-care systems, and the private sector promoted behavior change for prevention, provided a rapid emergency response in the short term, mitigated socioeconomic impacts of the pandemic, and built resilience for the future.

Scaling up support to strengthen climate resilience of the urban poor through an effective public health system will require addressing a range of gaps. First, a comprehensive understanding of the full spectrum of plausible health impacts of climate change, especially on the urban poor, remains limited. For example, the current national priorities on climate change adaptation do not pay much attention to health impacts due to heat stress and waterborne diseases, which are expected to affect the urban poor disproportionately considering the high-density and poor living conditions in which they typically reside.

Second, in the absence of such an understanding, interventions that can provide promotive and preventive functions to reduce the risk of such health impacts remain limited. Promotive and preventive functions operate *ex ante* and are useful in ensuring that vulnerable populations adopt the right health behaviors, access appropriate medical

advice, and receive the right treatments in advance of ill-health and disease. For example, in the context of climate change, increased awareness of managing health issues in advance of heat wave (e.g., optimal hydration regimens, protocols for ventilation of workplaces, ensuring regular contact with at-risk populations) can have a major impact on reducing heat-related mortality and morbidity. Similarly, promotive and preventive activities to limit the expansion of vectors for dengue and malaria can help reduce their spread.

Third, a key challenge in addressing health-related risks is the wider physical environment in which urban poor typically reside, with limited basic services, especially related to water and sanitation. For example, even though toilets are common among urban poor households, there are underlying problems such as the existence of non-science-based soak pits and/or septic tanks that often have to be manually cleaned and the fecal sludge removed and disposed on unused land or in water bodies.[64]

Building resilience to the health impacts of climate change would require a range of interventions, not limited to the health sector. Wider factors, such as deficit in basic infrastructure, improved governance, strengthened capacity for delivery at all levels including capacity (quality and number) of health workers, improved disaster preparedness and response, research and development, need to be addressed for public health systems to build the resilience of the urban poor, and the following actions from a climate resilience perspective will be critical:

• **Ensure climate risk considerations are recognized in health and related policy areas.** Various plans related to climate change and health need to recognize the importance of the full spectrum of plausible health impacts of climate change, including heat stress, especially

[61] S. Preuss. 2020. Indonesia and COVID-19: What the World Is Missing. *The Diplomat*. 24 April.
[62] Vaksinati Gotong Royong. 2021. About the Program.
[63] K. O'Rourke. 2021. The Trouble With Indonesia's Dual Track Vaccination Scheme. *The Diplomat*. 08 March.
[64] World Bank. 2017. Meeting Indonesia's Urban Sanitation Needs. Feature Story. 21 March.

on urban areas. It will also be important to understand the impacts on the health sector due to climate impacts on other sectors, such as food security, and water and sanitation. For example, with high levels of stunting and wasting, urban areas in Indonesia are in need of more focused interventions for improving food security for the urban poor, including through urban agricultural practices. This is especially important given the rural bias in a number of social protection schemes. A previous impact analysis of Raskin (rice for the poor) on staple food diversification in three rural communities in Central Java and Yogyakarta indicated that the government should regard staple food diversification as an adaptation strategy to climate change.[65] This has been taken into account in the National Action Plan on Food and Nutrition 2020–2024, which is currently under development. This new action plan emphasizes the importance of food safety and food security, including through food fortification, biofortification, food diversification, supervision of food products, and food and nutrition fortification. Moreover, a non-cash food assistance program also served as a social safety net approach for the vulnerable groups to help them access nutritious food. Such responses have the potential to enable transformational adaptation.

- **Strengthen institutional coordination to address climate change concerns in health.** The four key sectors included in PBI 2020-2045 have each been allocated to a ministry and as part of this, with the Ministry of Health charged with taking ownership of priorities on health. While several units with the Ministry of Health advance climate actions, including the Secretariat General, Directorate General of Disease Prevention and Control, and Directorate General of Public Health, it is critical to strengthen coordination between different units and to strengthen capacity, where required.

- **Use research and climate risk information to prioritize new public health infrastructure and programs that benefit the urban poor.** An important and immediate step would be to identify climate risk hot spots for urban areas (and within cities) in Indonesia and use the information to identify the current gaps in adequate health infrastructure in such hot spots. Climate and disaster risk databases described in section 4.2 can act as good starting points. Such an analysis would require collecting improved data on the impact that climate change will have specifically on the urban poor based on their typical living conditions and employment patterns. For example, "neighborhood effects" are common features of slums and create additional health burdens that need to be understood, if they are to be addressed.[66] The analysis should also look beyond dengue hemorrhagic fever and malaria to include issues of heat and occupational health, waterborne disease, and respiratory illnesses that will become more acute with climate change. Based on such an understanding, future health infrastructure and public health programs can be prioritized, thereby facilitating incremental adaptation. Equally important is to improve housing, basic services, and settlement programs, thereby addressing the underlying drivers of vulnerabilities and facilitating transformational adaptation. It should also inform future skills among health practitioners.

- **Improve multipurpose health early warning and surveillance systems.** It could include the expanded use of information and communication technology (ICT) to develop and strengthen health early warning and

65 A.W. Utami, L.A. Cramer, and N. Rosenberger. 2018. Staple Food Diversification Versus Raskin: Developing Climate Change Resilience in Rural Indonesia. *Human Organization*. 77 (4). pp. 359–370.

66 A. Ezeh, B. Mberu, and T. Haregu. 2016. Slum health is not urban health: why we must distinguish between the two. *The Conversation*. 19 December.

A primary health center (puskesmas) in Kelurahan Pekalipan, Cirebon City. Strengthening capacity of primary health-care services will be critical to deal with changing diseases patterns due to climate change.

surveillance systems that better predict the health impacts of climate events (such as the link between temperature rise and heat-related mortality and morbidity or extreme rainfall and the spread of infectious disease). Outputs from such systems can be linked to protocols used for triggering responses (e.g., cleaning drains to control disease vectors or establishing cooling centers in parts of a city that are badly affected). Improved early warning and surveillance system will provide a good basis to invest in promotive and preventive functions. Success of health early warning system would require close collaboration with local governments and different sector ministries. Such systems are also critical for responding to other shocks such as the current pandemic and facilitate coordinated response by various stakeholders

on health and social protection programs needed by the urban poor. With support from the World Bank, the government launched two mobile apps to prevent and handle COVID-19, as well as to deal with public health matters. The Village Against COVID-19 (Desa Melawan COVID-19) app will help village volunteers educate and provide the public with information on the outbreak, and collect real-time data on transmission and impact of COVID-19 on the community. The e-Human Development Worker (e-HDW) app will assist the Human Development Cadres (KPM) in monitoring both specific and sensitive nutrition interventions during the pandemic.[67]

67 Cabinet Secretariat of the Republic of Indonesia. 2020. Gov't Rolls Out Two Apps to Prevent, Handle COVID-19. 13 May.

- **Introduce new programs that deliver direct support for urban outdoor workers to address key occupational health and safety issues.** Outdoor workers are susceptible to heat stress, which can lead to short-term illness and longer-term disease. Many of these workers operate in the informal sector or are paid on a daily basis, so an inability to work also has a significant effect on livelihoods. Direct support for street vendors, street sweepers, and other outside workers can include assessing and improving the availability of drinking water (e.g., through public water fountains), the provision of accessible toilets (a particularly important issue for women), and sheds for street vendors. In the formal sector, employers can be mandated to provide appropriate support (e.g., requiring breaks if the temperature exceeds a certain level, providing water and appropriate protective clothing).

- **Enhance infrastructure resilience of health service facilities.** It is critical to strengthen the resilience of health-related physical infrastructure to ensure that health facilities accessed by vulnerable populations, including the urban poor, can continue providing services despite climate shocks and stresses. Identification of climate hot spots (described earlier) can include a geospatial database on health infrastructure information, including information that typically contributes to physical vulnerabilities of a structure. Such information can be used to prioritize retrofitting of existing infrastructure. Similarly, design, construction, and maintenance of new health infrastructure should factor resilience measures, thereby facilitating incremental adaptation. Equally important is to build the capacity of health services to better respond during disasters through improved ICT measures.

- **Increase focus on sanitation and waste management.** A focus on sanitation (see section 3.5 on SANIMAS) and waste management is crucial for enhancing the resilience of the urban poor and facilitate transformational adaptation. This will ensure a reduction of vectors for infectious disease (e.g., malaria and dengue) influenced by climate change and reduce the prevalence of diarrhea, malnutrition, and pneumonia. Examples and pilots of such initiatives exist, a good illustration of which comes from a resilience-building program in Semarang that entailed the improvement of a community-based sanitation system, increased awareness of the right domestic waste management practices, encouraged participatory construction of communal portable toilets and water purification systems, as well as work with the government to upgrade public sanitation facilities.[68] The requisite regulations to enable this activity exist.[69] A key focus of this initiative is community empowerment, with RPJMN 2020–2024 prioritizing community-based sanitation as a strategy for disease prevention and control.

- **Strengthen community awareness of the health impacts of climate change.** This may be done by scaling up awareness among the urban poor of the impacts of climate change on health, through a new curriculum on climate change and health in early education, through family development sessions part of social assistance program, through KSBs (see section 3.1) established by BNPB, and wider information dissemination and awareness-raising activities. It is also critical to raise awareness of health workers and decision-makers at central and regional levels on the impacts of climate change on health.

[68] Semarang City Government. 2016. *Resilient Semarang*.
[69] Regional Regulation No. 6/2012 on waste management and Regional Regulation No. 13/2006 on environment control.

Resilience through Safe Housing

Climate risk and housing for the urban poor. Only 2% of the national budget is dedicated to the development of affordable housing, which can cover only 30% of the country's housing needs. This amounts to a housing deficit of 7.63 million houses (in 2019), leaving 700,000 families on the lookout for affordable houses.[70] Thus, lack of affordable and quality housing is a major concern in urban areas of Indonesia. The location and quality of housing in the informal settlements is a key driver of risk for the urban poor. On average, more than 12% of the urban population lives in overcrowded housing. Related studies in the country reveal poor housing facilities as a main concern. Changes in climate will further increase the vulnerability of existing housing. Excess water from extreme precipitation events can lead to leaks and increased rusting of metallic components used in housing construction. Increased moisture in the air can also lead to increased growth of mold within buildings, which in turn could result in serious health impacts of the inhabitants. Extreme rainfall can also cause land subsidence that may damage the foundation of a building. Similarly, coastal inundation, where seawater impacts the built environment, can reduce the strength of building materials. Extreme heat can also severely damage shelter through the impact of thermal stress that can lead to the expansion and eventual buckling of metal and steel components that may not be designed to withstand high temperatures.[71] Related to housing is the issue of tenure. In Jakarta, over half of the land parcels are not registered and without a title, leaving residents vulnerable to eviction.[72] Lack of secure landownership disincentivizes households to invest in resilient building measures.

Safe and affordable housing is an essential component for building resilience of the urban poor. Physically, it means providing the urban poor with a safe, decent, and affordable shelter, thereby achieving a minimum standard of living. Socially, it represents being in a community or neighborhood, getting equal and fair access to basic services and secure tenure. Economically, housing provides stability, an asset to access credit. It also often provides space for home-based livelihoods. Environmentally, it represents shelter located in safe areas with provision of safe water, sanitation, and solid waste management, thus supporting hygiene and health. It also represents using appropriate building materials and technology that are environment-friendly and locally produced. Strengthening resilience through housing requires interventions in all four fronts in order to capture the true dividends. The interventions should include a package of measures: pro-poor policy on risk-informed upgrading, rehabilitation, and relocation; standards and regulations to promote resilient design and construction; subsidy to invest in retrofitting, rental housing, or employing climate-friendly building materials; housing microfinance; and promotion of community-driven approaches for construction.

A wide range of policies and programs provide a strong foundation for promoting resilient housing for the urban poor in Indonesia. At the broadest level, pro-poor housing-related policies include upgrading slum settlements, provision of new housing units for the poor, and resettlement of communities located in hazard-prone areas. Historically, a number of initiatives have been implemented to support these policies, such as the Kampung Improvement Program (KIP), Program Penanggulangan Kemiskinan di Perkotaan (P2KP), and Program Nasional Pemberdayaan Masyarakat

[70]   B. Ventura. 2019. Pemerintah Harus Perkuat Perumahan Rakyat dan Pembangunan Perkotaan (in Indonesian). SINDOnews.com. 30 August.

[71]   M. Nguyen, X. Wang, and D. Chen. 2011. An Investigation of Extreme Heatwave Events and Their Effects on Building and Infrastructure. CSIRO *Climate Adaptation Flagship Working paper* No. 9.

[72]   World Bank. 2011. *Jakarta: Urban Challenges in a Changing Climate*. Jakarta.

Subsidized housing. Safe and affordable housing like the one developed in Kelurahan, Kalijaga, Cirebon City, is an essential component for building resilience of the urban poor.

(PNPM) Mandiri–Perkotaan. Indonesia has an evolved institutional architecture for the provision of public housing, resettlement, and upgrading. The primary institution charged with providing public housing in Indonesia is Kementerian Pekerjaan Umum dan Perumahan Rakyat (PUPR), Ministry of Public Works and Human Settlement. Within PUPR, the Directorate General for Human Settlements and Directorate General for Housing are charged with delivering housing programs and policies for the urban poor. While the PUPR does not have an explicit focus on tackling climate change, it has undertaken programs to reduce the risk of flooding and improve water security.

PUPR is currently implementing the KOTAKU program to deliver 100% access to drinking water and sanitation and work toward slum-free cities. Even though addressing climate risk is not an explicit focus of the program, improved drainage, access to drinking water, and improved structural resilience of housing units delivered by this program help the urban poor deal with a variety of climate-induced shocks and stresses. There are also other programs supporting the urban poor. The Neighborhood Upgrading and Shelter Project

(NUSP-2) employs community engagement and public–private partnerships to improve housing and basic services. The Rehabilitasi Sosial Rumah Tidak Layak Huni (RS-Rutilahu) focuses on the renovation of houses for the urban poor by employing an innovative modality in that up to 15 adjacent households have to prepare a joint proposal for renovation and submit it to the government for funding. One member of the group making the application must have experience in building and construction, and a detailed report on renovations undertaken has to be submitted to the government within 100 days. There is also an example of resettlement programs that dealt with disasters, such as the successful Bengawan Solo River Resettlement, which resulted in relocating 1,571 households from Bengawan Solo Riverbank in 2008–2012 to form new communities within the city boundaries in the northern area of Mojosongo, which is not hazard prone.[73] This wide range of programs adopting different approaches including community-driven

---

[73] J. Taylor. 2015. A Tale of Two Cities: Comparing Alternative Approaches to Reducing the Vulnerability of Riverbank Communities in Two Indonesian Cities. *Environment and Urbanization.* 27 (2). pp. 621–636.

development, nature-based solutions, and blended finance provides a solid base for scaling up resilient housing for the urban poor in Indonesia. In addition, in 2015, the government committed to reducing the housing backlog as an explicit priority in the RPJMN and launched an ambitious initiative called Sejuta Rumah (One Million Homes), which included plans for building 5,257 twin apartment block towers for 515,711 families, social housing subsidies for 5.5 million households, improvements to 37,407 hectares of informal or inadequate housing areas, and the provision of government-supported credit facilities for 2.5 million low-income households.[74]

Scaling up climate-resilient housing for the urban poor would require addressing a host of challenges. First, slum upgrading initiatives often adopt in situ upgrades, but the focus is on those with formal tenure. Thus, a large number of the most vulnerable households who do not have secure land tenure are unable to benefit from these upgrading initiatives that have a crucial

bearing on reducing exposure and vulnerability to climate shocks and stresses.

Second, the eligibility criteria for enrollment in public housing programs remain important barriers for scaling up. A number of public housing programs prioritize housing for those who have the means to prove that they belong to the city or area where public housing is being developed and give preference to those who are considered to be "locals" in their respective communities. This automatically means that some of the most vulnerable sections of the urban poor, such as migrants, find it difficult to access these schemes.

Third, resettlement programs tend to be largely reactive after a major event such as a disaster.

Fourth, lack of synergy between different community-level programs, which at times are implemented in the same areas. Due to different institutional setups, these programs often work in parallel in an uncoordinated manner. This in turn leads to duplication, replication, extended timelines, and higher costs. A good example is the manner in which different slum upgrading and community infrastructure programs establish individual community groups (e.g., Badan Keswadayaan Masyarakat – BKM/LKM and Kelompok Siaga Bencana – KSB). This takes time and resources and creates competition for enrolling volunteers and community leaders from the same group of residents.

Fifth, a standardized model of public housing is a constraint. Due to the scale of the public housing challenge in the country, the government has adopted a broad-brush approach by developing a standard typology for public housing, which may not be appropriate to deal with different types of climate shocks and stresses faced in different urban areas.

Last, none of the major policies, plans, and programs related to housing and/or climate change

74   Oxford Business Group. 2018. *Housing Reform Set to Accelerate Development in Indonesian Construction.*

adaptation has an explicit attention to resilient housing for the poor.

Scaling up resilient housing for the urban poor requires a series of policy and program actions and adjustments to enable transformational change:

- **Undertake targeted policy shifts to promote transformational adaptation through the housing sector.** First, revisit policies and protocols for resettlement programs to ensure that this process takes place *ex ante* and that populations at risk are relocated before disaster events take place. Second, revise rules and protocols of informal settlement upgrade programs to include hazard considerations of site, tenure regularization, and simplified beneficiary targeting, which would help include a larger number of at-risk urban populations (especially migrants) within these vital schemes and programs. For example, the World Bank's City Planning Lab[75] developed a suitability tool for identifying locations for affordable in-city housing and analyzed 99 Fasilitas Likuiditas Pembiayaan Perumahan (FFLP or Housing Loan Liquidity Facility)[76] housing developments built in 2016 and 2017. Most subsidized houses in the sample were found to have low suitability index given their location in the outskirts of the city and in other suboptimal areas. Third, revisit public housing typologies to reflect location-specific climate risks as well as the highly diverse needs of the urban poor depending on their livelihood patterns and cultural background, and introduce technical specifications for housing design as well as retrofitting of housing. Fourth, explore the need for introducing subsidies to support the urban poor in dealing with climate shocks and stresses, including a rental subsidy for seasonal migrants, subsidy for purchase of climate-resilient housing construction material, and subsidy for owner-driven home retrofitting or construction. For example, the Self-Help Housing Stimulus (BSPS) introduced by the government in 2006 provides assistance to incremental self-built housing for households earning below Rp1.5 million ($113) per month. These households receive a subsidy of Rp10 million–Rp30 million ($751–$2,253) for home improvements or new construction. Such a scheme can easily mainstream resilient housing features through subsidies. Fifth, issue directives to strengthen the coordination between housing-related programs targeted at the poor, for example by establishing a single community institution that can support all the programs and also continue to function even after the programs conclude and be used by new programs in the future. This will ensure community understanding that climate risk is factored in program design and implementation, making it easier to provide targeted capacity-building support.

- **Mainstream climate and disaster risk considerations in the design and implementation of housing programs.** This would mean that government agencies leading these programs would need to institute risk assessment processes to inform site selection and, where necessary, improve site conditions such as through land stabilization in landslide-prone area; introduce measures to limit exposure to natural hazards such as through safeguards that housing units are based on plinths to reduce risk from floods; and reduce vulnerability such as through the provision of improved water and sanitation, introduction of new building material that can withstand heat, and rainwater harvesting systems to reduce the risk of water scarcity, thereby facilitating incremental adaptation. The ministries responsible for delivering particular programs

---

[75] M. Roberts, F. Gil Sander, and S. Tiwari. 2019. *Time to ACT: Realizing Indonesia's Urban Potential*. Washington, DC: World Bank.
[76] Offers concessional funding to lending entities who provide mortgages at fixed interest rates, i.e., 5% yearly over 20 years. Government and participating banks fund 90% and 10% liquidity, respectively.

could issue enforceable regulations to strengthen resilience. For example, Perda Rumah Panggung has mandated the use of stilts for houses built within the Banjarmasin for riverbank communities. Technical manuals can also guide the integration of disaster risk considerations in housing design. Recognizing the importance of informal builders for upgrading slums, the ministries could provide training in climate-resilient building practices. Moreover, the institution of regional regulations (i.e., perda) and their enforcement at the city level for ensuring that building designs take climate and disaster risk considerations into account could provide strong incentives for mainstreaming climate risk in housing development. These regulations need to also apply to private sector developments and policies, such as Zero Delta Q (mentioned in Government Regulation No. 26/2008 on National Spatial Planning), which mandate the control of surface runoff for all new building developments and need to be communicated to developers and enforced.

· **Strengthen coordination between housing and land use and infrastructure programs.** Building resilient communities and households will require coordination of efforts between urban land use planning, community- and city-scale infrastructure provision, and housing development. For example, in the context of relocation programs, it is important to ensure wider linkages with urban spatial planning processes to take into account the issues of urban sprawl and of limiting impact on agriculture land and forest areas, thereby advancing transformational adaptation. This may require coordination across administrative boundaries if there are serious limitations to available land in particular locations. Similarly, links should be established between housing programs and local disaster preparedness planning processes.

· **Promote housing microfinance for construction and retrofitting of housing.** Housing microfinance should be promoted to support urban poor households in constructing resilient new housing, retrofitting existing houses, and repairing and rebuilding housing damaged by disasters. Such programs should combine access to finance with technical assistance on construction, retrofitting, and repair using resilient design features. KPRS/KPRS Mikro Bersubsidi, which designed for low-income groups to access a subsidy for home improvement, offers an opportunity to integrate home improvements to combat disasters and the impacts of climate change. Support could include strengthening a capital base for housing microfinance institutions, through programs such as the Housing Financing Liquidity Facility (FLPP) and Interest Rate Buy-Down Subsidy (SSB),[77] in order to support the urban poor, establishing a special refinance scheme that ensures housing resilience and setting up a risk-sharing facility to cater to low-income households who choose to invest in resilient housing.

· **Facilitate private sector engagement in resilient pro-poor housing.** First, the public sector can offer a range of subsidies to commercially incentivize the private sector to deliver affordable housing options to the market. These include land cross-subsidization through land rights or income mixing, cost recoveries through annuities, capital grants, transfer of asset ownership, and asset rental. Within such collaborations, the public sector has the opportunity to include resilient housing designs in the local context. Government efforts to provide incentives to the private sector through Rusunami[78] initiatives by introducing waivers on transfer tax to developers selling affordable

---

[77] Provides subsidy to cover the difference between the commercial loan interest rate and the subsidized flat 5% rate in a given loan term.

[78] Public rental program for beneficiaries earning below the provincial minimum wage, with a nationwide qualifying income limit of Rp2.5 million ($187) a month.

housing below Rp144.0 million ($10,814), could extend to builders and developers for delivering resilient housing. Second, land and property tax can be used as a tool to invest in resilient housing for the poor. For example, Tax Incremental Financing can attract private sector to invest in resilient housing.[79] The rationale for this tool is to use future gains for future improvements. For instance, the value of housing with resilient features is higher when the investments incurred for incorporating the resilient features into these housing can benefit the local government through increased taxes on the higher property value of resilient housing. This increased tax amount can be redirected to investors or the private sector, or it can be allocated for other projects. Third, land value capture[80] or transfer of development rights, are alternatives to attract the private sector to resilient housing through clear incentives and regulations such as subsidies in developer levies or fees, incentive schemes, and capital works schemes in new developments. Cross-subsidization for building resilient housing can be tested using mechanisms that have been tried out in Indonesia, such as the Tanjung Barat project where national affordable housing developer, Perumnas, partnered with the state-owned railway enterprise, PT KAI Commuter Jabodetabek, to develop a housing project in the Jakarta multidistrict metro area, whereby Perumnas will build 650 apartment units, 10% of which will be affordable and eligible for a national subsidy under the FLPP. The profits from the market-rate apartments will be used to build affordable houses in other regions of the country. Fourth, the government can encourage the use of resilient building construction materials by provide a matching line of credit designed to incentivize suppliers to produce sustainable building materials that

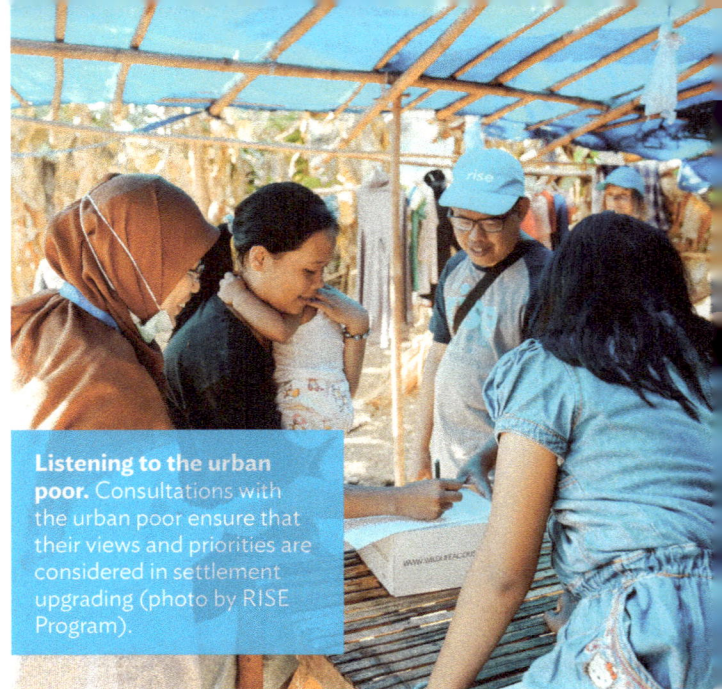

Listening to the urban poor. Consultations with the urban poor ensure that their views and priorities are considered in settlement upgrading (photo by RISE Program).

are innovative and resistant to disasters and the impact of climate change. The government can also ensure that the use of innovative resilient building materials is integrated in urban planning regulations and building codes for resilient housing.

- **Explore alternative models for delivering resettlement and upgrading.** The current set of approaches for resettlement and upgrading suffer from an uneven amount of public participation. A more concerted effort is needed to ensure that the views and priorities of the urban poor are taken on board to a greater degree in all such programs through iterative, multi-stakeholder dialogues that attempt to include the views of the full spectrum of the urban poor through robust community organizations. Such views are critical to understand the vulnerabilities in the context of changing climate risk. New models and approaches such as community-led resettlement and land purchase initiatives and in situ participatory redevelopment of resilient housing should also be actively considered as they provide opportunities for transformational adaptation. In essence, policies and programs need to recognize that housing and settlements are a social process, with communities at the center and not merely a product.

[79]   L. Walters. 2011. *Land and Property Tax: A Policy Guide.* Nairobi: United Nations Human Settlements Programme (UN-Habitat).

[80]   City Resilience Program - World Bank Group. n.d. Land Value Capture: Investment in Infrastructure. PowerPoint presentation.

Resilience through Robust Community Infrastructure

Climate impacts on urban basic services. With rapid urbanization, urban areas have not been able to meet the growing demand for infrastructure particularly in informal settlements where many of the poor reside. Limited access to electricity, water, sanitation, and drainage are some of the major concerns of informal settlements in Indonesia. More than 30% of the urban poor do not have access to safe drinking water. Water quality remains of particular concern, especially in peri-urban areas due to close proximity of surface and household drainage systems. Climate modeling points to increased water scarcity in Indonesia over the next decades. In 2010, 14% of the country's 453 districts recorded no months of surplus water. This is projected to increase to 20% by 2025 and 31% by 2050.[81] The urban poor often rely on rainwater for non-potable use. Climate change will alter the rainfall pattern, affecting the quantity of rainwater available to the urban poor. Similarly, overreliance on retail water (sold through water trucks and kiosks) for daily consumption poses a financial burden to the poor. Moreover, in many parts of Indonesia, large extraction of groundwater has led to land subsidence. Sea level rise driven by climate change will likely result in greater saltwater intrusion over the next century,[82] which will have an impact on water resources. Thus, PBI 2020–2045 recognizes water security as a critical topic for dealing with climate risk. The RPJMN 2020–2024 has recognized the importance of climate- and disaster-resilient infrastructure, including combining gray and green infrastructure, implementing integrated watershed management for strengthening flood risk, adopting a combination of structural and non-structural solutions for strengthening resilience, and establishing an early warning system.

Robust and integrated infrastructure is critical for strengthening resilience of the urban poor. The urban poor rely on community infrastructure for their basic needs, thereby making it critical to ensure that such infrastructure (i) is *robust*—designed, constructed, and managed to withstand the physical impacts of natural hazards without significant damage or loss of functions; (ii) builds in *redundancy*—spare capacity and diversity to accommodate disruption, including disruption of climate shocks; and (iii) is a result of *integrated* planning, which recognizes the dependency among and between community infrastructure and wider trunk infrastructure. It is also essential that such infrastructure promote sustainability, especially source sustainability, such as in the case of sustainable sources of water supply to ensure long-term availability. In addition, there is growing recognition of the need to protect, sustainably manage, and restore natural ecosystems, which play a critical role in resilience and are a valid alternative for engineered infrastructure.

Community infrastructure, especially water supply and sanitation, has been an important part of Indonesia's urban poverty reduction programs. Examples include the Program Nasional Pemberdayaan Masyarakat (PNPM) Mandiri-Perkotaan; the PAMSIMAS—Community-based Drinking Water Supply and Sanitation, which has supported 17 million people through improved water supply and sanitation and promotion of hygiene measures such as handwashing; the SANIMAS program aimed at providing community sanitation; the Neighborhood Upgrading and Shelter Project (NUSP) working with local governments in 20 cities to improve infrastructure and public service delivery for 670,000 households in underserved communities; the KOTAKU National Slum

---

[81] Government of Indonesia. 2020. Second national communication to UNFCCC.

[82] N. Rahmawati, J.F. Vuillaume, and I.L.S. Purnama. 2013. Salt Intrusion in Coastal and Lowland Areas of Semarang City. *Journal of Hydrology*, 494, pp. 146–159. https://www.sciencedirect.com/science/article/pii/S0022169413003259?via%3Dihub

Box 3: Enhancing Community Resilience through the Introduction of Nature-Based Solutions in Informal Settlements in Makassar

Residents of informal settlements are resilient. Evidence of this resilience is everywhere. In a small settlement in the district of Batua in Makassar, residents have come together every wet season to fund bamboo rafts and walkways to cope with the floods that engulf their homes for days at a time. These coping strategies are critical in supporting families to meet their daily needs among the many pressures and challenges that arise living in informal settlements.

The Revitalizing Informal Settlements and their Environments (RISE) Program, supported by the Asian Development Bank through the Urban Climate Change and Resilience Trust Fund, is assisting thousands of households living in informal settlements with water and sanitation improvements.

The RISE Program focuses on neighborhood-scale nature-based solutions such as constructed wetlands and biofilters, together with more traditional "gray" infrastructure to provide a holistic, water-sensitive approach to improving services in urban informal settlements. It aims to reduce fecal contamination in the environment and, by doing so, reduce human exposure to pathogens. The program includes interventions at a range of scales to address water supply, drainage, sanitation, flood management, and access challenges. At its heart is the codesign of infrastructure solutions, together with each community, to ensure the solutions are fit for purpose.[a]

Engaging with the community. A community facilitator explains the role of plants in green infrastructure to community residents in Makassar, Indonesia as part of the co-design process for the RISE program (photo by RISE Program).

Without the availability of citywide networks for water and sanitation, people are exposed to contamination in and around their homes because of poor sanitation and drainage, and often a lack of appropriate quality and quantity of water to meet their daily needs. Residents are acutely aware of many of the health impacts they face, as well as their causes, with few avenues for them to pursue to effect change.

The Urban Climate Change Resilience Trust Fund seeks to improve the livability of cities and harness the power of existing social support networks, and the resilience of the residents, to work together to deliver a holistic, water-sensitive solution within the context of existing constraints, and taking into account each community's future aspirations and plans.

Understanding the broader link to the health and well-being of residents is a key objective of the RISE Program, which will follow the health of residents to understand how a holistic approach to upgrading urban services might benefit individual households and their resilience.

---

[a]   Burge, K., et al. 2020. Gotong Royong: Unity and Resilience in Makassar's Informal Settlements amid a Pandemic. Livable Cities, Asian Development Bank.
Source: Asian Development Bank.

Upgrading Program, which aims to improve access to water, sanitation, and drainage in 154 cities in Indonesia; and the newly initiated Revitalizing Informal Settlement and their Environments (RISE), which adopts a "water sensitive" approach to provide flood protection measures, rainwater harvesting, improved drainage, and the restoration of water ways and green open spaces that help build resilience of the urban poor in 12 settlements in Makassar (Box 3). Some of these programs, such as the NSUP also includes relocation projects for households affected by large-scale infrastructure projects, such as a flood-prone neighborhood affected by a riverbank clearing project in Bima. Moving forward, community infrastructure remains a priority under the RPJMN 2020–2024, which targets at providing 10 million connections to improve clean water access, to achieve 100% clean water coverage and 90% sanitation access respectively. With respect to climate change, PBI 2020–2045 identifies water as one of four priority sectors as well as the need to develop water storage infrastructures, rehabilitate water catchment areas, apply water recycling and reclamation technology, reinforce regulations on water resource management, and capacitate communities on optimal use of water resources in order to prevent water shortages.

Community infrastructure projects in Indonesia have often adopted community-driven approaches for implementation, which is critical for strengthening resilience. The PNPM Mandiri included active community involvement in formulating and prioritizing community infrastructure based on community risk mapping. The KOTAKU uses a participatory community approach to alleviate conditions in informal settlements, working in collaboration with local governments. The NUSP has a strong focus on community engagement. The RISE program has adopted a participatory planning process with community members for designing green infrastructure solutions. Also, in order to ensure the sustainability of the infrastructure, the PAMSIMAS included community-based

associations that can manage and finance the facilities. Community-driven approaches have also been used successfully in the context of post-disaster reconstruction, such as after the 2004 Indian Ocean Tsunami. The households displaced by the disaster were involved in the rebuilding process, from negotiating redrawn land boundaries to physical reconstruction. This helped ensure that the reconstruction was tailored to the needs of the affected communities. It also enabled certain households, such as widows, to be prioritized through a collective, more acceptable decision-making process.

Community-driven approaches are also common in programs supported by nongovernment organizations. One example is in Yogyakarta where informal riverside settlements have been upgraded using revolving city-level loans and an Asian Coalition for Community Action (or ACCA) grant to provide loans to families for infrastructure upgrading (improving riverside walkways) and housing improvements. This demonstrated an alternative strategy for improving these riverside settlements in a way which ends river encroachment and builds resilience through better housing and infrastructure. The process also addressed the problem of insecurity of tenure, as the community negotiated the right to stay on the government land they already occupied, aligning with the local government plans to solve the problems of riverside *kampungs* in the whole of Yogyakarta.[83] Thus, such a community-driven approach is critical from a resilience perspective as it brings about local understanding of climate risk; promotes inclusive decision-making; ensures longer-term sustainability of assets through community ownership and maintenance; and helps build longer-term relationship between communities and local government, which is essential to address difficult issues related to land, tenure, and encroachment.

83 Asian Coalition for Housing Rights. 2014. *ACHR and Indonesia.*

Several challenges exist in strengthening resilience of community infrastructure. Despite the increase in Indonesia's ranking in infrastructure competitiveness, the country faces a wide range of infrastructure-relates issues, including availability and coverage, quality, and funding. Urban areas are not free from such issues; in fact, the high rate of urbanization puts further pressure on an already limited and weak infrastructure system. Specific to climate resilience, the following challenges stand out.

First, the current focus on infrastructure and associated targets do not necessarily consider longer-term changes in climate. For example, the large focus on access to clean water includes rainwater, spring water, and retail water brought from water trucks. However, changing climate patterns may impact the reliability (quality and quantity) of water sources, even if access is in place. Increase in water scarcity will impact the urban poor's ability to harvest rainwater and will increase their financial burden with the need to rely on retail water. Similarly, groundwater extraction can lead to negative environmental impacts. For example, the land subsidence rate is very high in the coastal areas, where massive groundwater extraction from PAMSIMAS is considered a main cause. This high rate increases the risks faced by coastal communities that are already at risk from tidal flooding, by creating permanently inundated settlement areas. Sea level rise and high-intensity flash floods will worsen the matter, with all hazards culminating in one location.[84]

Second, understanding of the impact of climate risk on the wider infrastructure system is limited. Different programs focus on different infrastructure. While each has the potential to strengthen resilience, if not planned holistically, they can inadvertently increase vulnerability. It is also not enough to strengthen just one piece of infrastructure, but to look at the entire system.

For example, addressing flooding in coastal urban areas may require a suite of measures including improvement of drainage, elevation of road, sea wall construction, conservation of the coastal ecosystem, improved zoning regulations, disaster preparedness planning, and operation and maintenance of infrastructure. Each of these measures might fall under the responsibility of different organizations.

Third, communities and local governments have limited capacity in operation and maintenance of infrastructure, especially the ones that adopt new technology such as desalination plants.

Fourth, limited meaningful participatory planning processes pose a challenge in prioritizing local resilience-building needs. The *Musrenbangda* – Local Development Planning Deliberation is participatory in nature but, at times, is tightly controlled by political elites and vested interests.[85] This poses a challenge for the urban poor particularly in ensuring that their priorities are accommodated and highlighted within this crucially important decision-making process. As a result, the development of community infrastructure for the most vulnerable has largely been overlooked. For instance, poor residents of the Kelurahan Rawa Buaya have been highlighting the need to restore and improve a malfunctioning drainage system at the community level, but this has not received due attention within the *Musrenbangda* process. Thus, the community has had to pool resources to develop an ad hoc and incomplete solution to the problem without engaging the authorities.[86]

[84] Tribun Jateng. 2019. *Moratorium of New Deep Well by Pekalongan Regency* (in Indonesian). 30 August.

[85] M. Ford, ed. 2013. *Social Activism in Southeast Asia.* Abingdon, UK: Routledge.

[86] Kompas.com. 2008. *Musrenbang Is Deemed as Ineffective to Gather Aspiration.*

Community infrastructure for poverty reduction. The communal wastewater treatment plant (IPAL) and a public toilet facility (MCK Komunal) funded by Islamic Development Bank in Kelurahan Kasepuhan, Cirebon City, are examples of community infrastructure implemented through a poverty reduction program.

Implementing resilient community infrastructure requires moving away from business-as-usual planning and implementation and undertaking the following measures:

- **Ensure climate-resilient water management principles guide the delivery of basic services aimed at the urban poor.** This would entail a shift away from a heavy reliance on groundwater as the primary source of water; the development of structures and approaches for the optimal utilization of rainwater and enhanced filtration of river and spring water; and capacity-building of community-based actors and organizations in the monitoring and supply of water within informal settlements. The approaches being trialed in the RISE project

for rainwater harvesting and biofiltration of water, implemented with community planning, could be examples for scaling up and enabling transformational adaptation. This will build the resilience of the urban poor by improving both the quality of water and the consistency of its supply, including under conditions of water stress. A neighborhood-level participatory mapping of water-related challenges (e.g., availability, quality) and potential opportunities for alleviating these challenges (e.g., developing community-based water harvesting infrastructure) can help in adopting such an approach. This is essential to provide a granular understanding of key issues that can be collated into a strategic approach for enhancing the resilience of the water sector in urban areas at scale. This needs

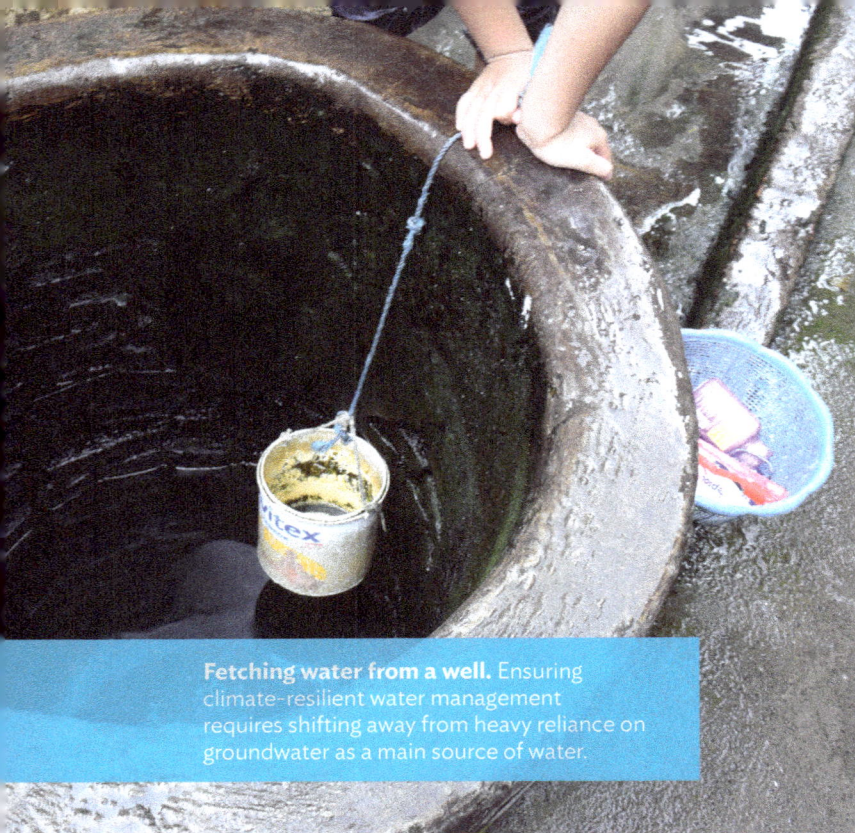

Fetching water from a well. Ensuring climate-resilient water management requires shifting away from heavy reliance on groundwater as a main source of water.

to be supplemented by community mapping and enumeration processes involving the urban poor in order to plan upgrading interventions, to ensure measures meet the needs of this group and are also climate resilient. However, the resilience of the water sector cannot be built by focusing only at the neighborhood level. It is therefore vital that interregional planning is employed at the scale of the watershed (that cuts across municipal boundaries) to find comprehensive and holistic solutions for augmenting water supply and managing the impact of water-related extreme events. Local communities should also be kept informed of water management approaches being applied on a watershed level and what actions they can take locally to support these approaches. This is particularly important for the urban and peri-urban poor who live in some of the most affected watershed locations.

· **Integrate climate risk considerations in PAMSIMAS planning and implementation. Local governments need to prepare a feasibility study for accessing resources from PAMSIMAS.** This study should factor in the impact of climate variability and change on water resources of the area to determine

the long-term reliability of a proposed water source and the potential adverse effects of accessing water from the source (including effects in downstream communities, potential land subsidence, saltwater intrusion), identify potential resilience qualities that need to be integrated in infrastructure design, and categorize the type of capacity-building and awareness-raising measures to be carried out to improve the understanding of the local community on climate risk and the operation and maintenance of proposed infrastructure facilities. SIDIK and Disaster Risk Index can be used along with hydrological analysis to inform such decisions along with information of the risk as perceived by the local communities. For example, in areas at risk from floods and drought, a combination of surface water (river) and groundwater sources can be selected. Excess surface water during floods can be stored for use during dry seasons. Such strategies may also require additional infrastructure not typically covered by the program. For example, typically PAMSIMAS finances pumping stations, elevated reservoirs, and household connection. However, to deal with floods and water scarcity may require water storage infrastructure and water treatment facilities. It will also be crucial to determine the social acceptability of proposed resilience measures through consultations with communities and build the capacity of communities for operation and maintenance. A key objective of PAMSIMAS is to inculcate behavior change within communities in respect to water, sanitation, and hygiene. This objective is key for facilitating transformational change by influencing sustainable and climate risk-informed practices on water management, sanitation, and hygiene.

· **Improve planning and implementation of the SANIMAS program from a climate risk perspective.** Based on community-driven development principles, SANIMAS provides wastewater infrastructure, including communal septic tanks, community bathing, washing and toilet blocks, and communal sewer treatment facilities for the crowded urban slum populations. Similar to PAMSIMAS, the planning process of SANIMAS includes a feasibility study and land acquisition. Climate risk considerations including SIDIK data, Disaster Risk Index, and community perception of risk should inform this process including the selection of resilient design features. For example, floating toilets could be considered for poor households residing in flood-prone areas. Domestic wastewater treatment facilities can also be used to turn influent wastewater into non-potable water for communities living in drought-prone areas. Building the capacity of communities, local government, and its water and sanitation utilities to operate and maintain such infrastructure will be important. One criterion for selecting communities for SANIMAS support includes the availability of a city sanitation strategy, which is important to ensure the citywide sanitation infrastructure is resilient at a systems level.

- **Enhance design considerations of the KOTAKU program to deliver on resilience.** The design of KOTAKU can be enhanced to move beyond the provision of basic services and beautification infrastructure to include discrete measures that have a primary purpose of building climate resilience, such as a combination of gray and green infrastructure to deal with flood risk. Site-specific climate risk and vulnerability assessment should be undertaken using SIDIK data and Disaster Risk Index and community perception of risk to identify infrastructure-related priorities for resilience-building and its relationship with existing development control regulations such as zoning regulations. Nature-based solutions such as water-sensitive urban landscape design and drainage systems, measures for landslide protection, and safe evacuation options can be promoted. Experiences can be drawn from the Gerakan Pengurangan Resiko Bencana program

implemented by BNPB and BPBD and efforts to increase the capacity of communities to reduce disaster risk by promoting nature-based solutions, such as urban farming, beach cleaning, and mangrove planting.

- **Link community infrastructure to wider risk-informed spatial plans.** The planned community infrastructure, including to reduce risk, such as drainage, seawalls, and groundwater extraction, should be aligned with and connected to existing or planned city- and regency-scale infrastructure by the local government, as well as with the spatial pattern and zoning regulations. Climate and disaster risk information should guide such land use management processes. While attempts have been made to mainstream climate risk considerations in spatial planning processes, the results remain limited due to a range of factors, including limited availability of the climate scenario, lack of local capacity in undertaking climate risk assessments, and limited coordination among different agencies that need to use the results of the risk assessment. The principles of disaster risk assessment also are integrated in the spatial structure plan (*rencana struktur ruang*) and spatial pattern plan (*rencana pola ruang*), but challenges related to data, scale, and capacity exist. Thus, it is critical to build technical capacity at the local level to undertake climate and disaster risk assessments and use the results of such assessments to inform pro-poor urban development strategies and formulate development control regulations (including zoning maps that can limit the exposure of urban informal settlements to natural hazards) to improve disaster preparedness through contingency plans. Such maps and plans should be made available to the public to influence household decisions. Where available, efforts should be made to link with related initiatives such as the Pengembangan Desa/Kelurahan Tangguh Bencana – DESTANA/KATANA (Development of Disaster Resilient

Village/Neighborhood), an initiative led by BNPB, which supports the development and implementation of neighborhood contingency plans through community-based disaster preparedness groups. Efforts should also be made to link community infrastructure with wider resilience-building programs such as the Urban Flood Resilience Programme and wider efforts to strengthen skills in the construction industry.

Box 4: **Women-Operated Decentralized Water Treatment Schemes as Strategic Investments in Climate Resilience**[a]

The availability of safe water is a prerequisite for economic growth and poverty reduction, as it is necessary for a number of life-sustaining and economic activities.[b] Indonesia is drawing closer to universal coverage to access to improved water sources in cities.[c] However, a 2017 water quality survey found that nearly all improved water sources have 77% to 90% contamination of *E.coli*, thus posing a serious and potentially widespread problem in urban poor settlements.[d] These issues would be compounded by climate change due to seawater intrusion from sea level rise, flooding, and groundwater contamination. For such a basic need, safe water is expensive due to its relative scarcity. Current regulations also place the burden on households to treat water before drinking (footnote d). Being the primary managers of water supply in the household, it is women who are greatly affected by water scarcity and quality problems and have higher stakes in resilience-building solutions. In this light, women-operated decentralized water treatment schemes appear as strategic investments on building climate resilience. Such women-focused investments must address gender-based vulnerabilities and aim for transformational change.

Women-operated decentralized water treatment schemes can create a value chain that includes production, servicing, marketing, distribution, and selling of clean drinking water in urban communities. The Climate Village Program (Proklim) may provide a platform for such investments given support from government, strong sense of local ownership, and active involvement of community women's groups in Proklim operations. The business model engages women in all stages of water treatment—from forming a social enterprise, investing in purification technologies, water treatment, to distribution and sale of clean drinking water—and diverges from conventional gender mainstreaming approaches. As women are to drive the cycle through, they also receive the full benefit by freeing their time, diversifying their livelihood, increasing their income, and improving their and their families' health. Their profits may also be reinvested in other productive enterprises in the community, generating long-term benefits for many. This project model develops women entrepreneurs and community leaders. This may serve not only to changes women's perspective of their own power and place, but also the view of other people as to the status of women in society, from passive beneficiaries to vigorous contributors to resilient development.

---

[a] This entire section draws heavily from this publication: ADB. 2020. *Enhancing Women-Focused Investments in Climate and Disaster Resilience*.
[b] Word Health Organization. 2019. *Drinking-water*.
[c] Statistics Indonesia. 2021. *Housing Statistics: Percentage of Households, by Province, Area Type, and Source of Improved Drinking Water*. Dynamic table.
[d] World Bank. 2017. Improving Service Levels and Impact on the Poor: *A Diagnostic of Water Supply, Sanitation, Hygiene, and Poverty in Indonesia*. WASH Poverty Diagnostic. World Bank, Washington, DC.

Enabling Resilience of the Urban Poor

Building resilience of the urban poor requires integrated and complementary interventions across a range of policy areas and at different scales (household, community, and citywide) following the principles of subsidiarity. As discussed in Chapter 3, overcoming current gaps and enabling resilience actions in specific policy areas requires risk-informed and inclusive governance; climate, disaster, and poverty data; and secured finance. These factors provide the enabling environment for securing and sustaining resilience and are also critical for facilitating innovation and partnerships needed for scaling up resilience. This chapter discusses these enabling factors.

Keeping households informed. Community facilitators of the RISE Program engage with residents participating in the program (pre-COVID-19) to ensure that they have the latest information on the project (photo by RISE Program).

Risk-Informed and Inclusive Governance in Support of Resilience

Governance is arguably the single most important enabler for enhancing the resilience of the urban poor. Urban governance (and the associated formal and informal processes) refers to the many ways in which institutions and individuals organize the day-to-day management of a city, as well as the processes used for effectively realizing short- and long-term development agendas, including legal frameworks, political, managerial, and administrative processes.[87] Key to good urban governance is a shared understanding of the roles and responsibilities across all tiers of government, coupled with an appropriate distribution of resources.[88] Collaboration with all relevant stakeholders—public institutions, private organizations, civil society, and citizens—needs to be supported and strengthened to offer opportunities for dialogue with and contributions from all segments of society.

Good urban governance is critical for shaping the way in which urban poverty and climate and disaster risk are addressed in decision-making and programming. Governance influences tenure security, access and operations of basic infrastructure and services, delivery of social protection, and livelihood support, all of which have a critical bearing on risk and resilience. Similarly, urban governance has a significant role in integrating programs and activities across policy areas and different scales (individual, household, neighborhood, city, national), which is of major importance in building urban resilience more broadly—and resilience of the urban poor in particular. Good governance recognizes the importance of civil engagement and participation, including the empowerment of citizens (especially women) and the recognition and support of the civil capital of the poor,[89] which is equally critical in terms of understanding vulnerabilities (including gendered vulnerabilities) and adopting a whole-of-society approach to strengthen resilience.

Indonesia has a well-developed and sophisticated system of local governance. Indonesia adopted a far-reaching decentralization policy in 1999 that grants vast powers to local and district governments. The decentralization policy gave authority to two levels of regional government—provinces (*provinsi*) at the first-order administrative level, and regencies (*kabupaten*) and municipalities (*kota*) at the second-order administrative level—to make their own policies and local bylaws, as well as to manage the budget and to implement local development initiatives.[90] The promise of greater autonomy led to the creation of new administrative units. Prior to decentralization, there were 26 provinces and 299 regencies and municipalities. Now Indonesia comprises 34 provinces subdivided into 416 regencies and 98 municipalities. These municipalities are further divided into 7,210 subdistricts, 74,957 villages, and thousands of *kelurahans* (following the establishment of Law No. 6 Year 2014, the villages have more authority to enact certain local policies and manage their own budget).[91] Local government functions relate to basic services, including education, health, public works and spatial planning, public housing,

---

[87] United Nations. 2016. Policy Paper 4: Urban Governance, Capacity and Institutional Development. Preparatory Committee for the United Nations Conference on Housing and Sustainable Urban Development, Habitat III.

[88] World Bank. 2001. Understanding Good Urban Governance and Management. Urban and City Management Program—Workbook Session 1 and 2.

[89] UN-Habitat: What is Good Governance?

[90] Law No. 22/1999 on Fiscal Balance between the Central Government and the Regional Governments.

[91] See "Profil Administrasi Wilayah Indonesia per Provinsi tahun 2017" in Data Statistik Desentralisasi dan Otonomi Daerah, Direktorat Otonomi Daerah, BAPPENAS, Jakarta 2018.

public order, and social affairs—all of which have a bearing on risk.[92]

Local governments have increased autonomy in urban development issues over the past 2 decades. The Regional Governance Law (22/1999) devolved considerable power to Indonesia's regions; this was complemented by the Fiscal Balance Law (25/1999) that gave them revenue sources and expenditure functions. Subsequent revisions of these laws (32/2004 and 33/2004) further strengthened provincial governments' coordination powers, and district governments became the chief providers of most public services including education, health, and infrastructure.[93] In sum, city management for the first time became the authority of subnational, rather than national, government. Still, urban stakeholders lacked the adequate capacity to manage land and municipal assets.[94] Similarly, infrastructure and investment policies were not sensitive to urban disparities, which resulted from the imbalanced concentration of people in Java and its cities. Affordable housing supply was regularly assigned without due consideration of the mobility patterns of the poorest Indonesians, and many were therefore pushed out to the urban periphery (footnote 79). High land costs in urban centers had a similar effect. These factors contribute to increased exposure and vulnerabilities of the urban poor.

Civil society is important in the pursuit of pro-poor policy outcomes in Indonesia, particularly at the subnational level. Decentralization opened space for non-state actors to play a more significant role in policy making. Indonesia implements a bottom-up participatory planning process called the *Musrenbang*, where communities from village and Kelurahan levels are invited to express their needs

and aspirations through a hierarchical process going all the way to the national level. This also creates space for the participation of CSOs in local governance processes. By August 2017, there were an estimated 350,000 CSOs[95] working in Indonesia across various sectors including the environment, women's rights, education, democratic governance, agriculture, and health.[96] A good example of one such organization is Uplink (Urban Poor Linkage), a major civil society network that focuses on pro-poor development in Indonesian cities (footnote 96). Uplink is now a national coalition of community-based organizations and NGOs and contributed to reconstruction efforts after the Indonesian tsunami of 2004.[97] Uplink facilitates knowledge sharing and works with community groups to encourage better pro-poor policy making at the city and national level (footnote 83). In addition, the government can enhance partnerships with a large number of NGOs that are operating in the urban space.

Integrated and collaborative governance in urban areas (essential for resilience) faces a few important hurdles. First, central, provincial and local government are assigned certain roles on urban issues, but there is no single entity or body at each level which is responsible for overall coordination and ensuring that results are achieved (footnote 94). Such lack of single coordination makes it difficult to understand if decisions at different scale are collectively contributing to resilience. Furthermore, there is a potential for better institutional alignment between national ministries and sectoral departments at the subnational level. For example, the Ministry of Public Works and Human Settlement is in charge of designing and developing infrastructure projects for the provision of water and then hands

---

92   Article 12, Law No. 23/2014 on Local Governance.
93   World Bank. 2005. *Urban Sector Development Reform Project.* Washington, DC. p. 3.
94   World Bank. 2009. *Indonesia Development Policy Review: Enhancing Government Effectiveness in a Democratic and Decentralised Indonesia.* Washington, DC.

95   Ministry of Home Affairs, Republic of Indonesia. 2017. *Kementerian Dalam Negeri R.I.* Jakarta.
96   World Bank. 2019. *Engaging with Civil Society in the Health Sector in Indonesia.* Washington, DC.
97   A.K. Jha. 2010. *Safer Homes, Stronger Communities; A Handbook for Reconstructing after Natural Disasters.* Washington, DC: World Bank. p. 277.

these over to utilities at the subnational level for the day-to-day management and delivery of services. However, this handover process is fractured and sometimes results in the inability of the utilities to usefully deliver services to the local level.[98] Participation in project development by implementers and enhanced operation and maintenance of services are critical in dealing with issues related to changes in climate.

Second, Law No. 23/2014 on Regional Administration mandates that district governments are responsible for delivering services within their geographically defined jurisdictions. The challenge, however, is that urban areas over the years have come to span multiple districts creating a need for a more unified approach toward the management of critical urban services. For example, the Jakarta Greater Area (JABODETABEK) is spread over 14 districts in three provinces, creating a substantial coordination challenge. Even though Law No. 23/2014 places responsibility for coordinating multidistrict areas with the provincial government, many are unable to perform this function because regulations are outdated and information on accountability and

funding mechanisms is scarce (footnote 98). This has direct implications on risk and resilience which are not necessarily contained within administrative boundaries and thereby require regular greater coordination.

Third, no national institution is explicitly responsible for urban development, nor does a coordination mechanism for urban issues exist. Rather, urban development is shared among a number of agencies and ministries that bear responsibility for different sectors (see table on page 68) (footnote 98). Without such a coordination mechanism, planning for resilience becomes difficult.

A number of ministries and agencies have the potential to better support the coordination processes to enhance the resilience of the urban poor. Apart from sector ministries that are responsible for the design and implementation of programs related to social protection, urban livelihoods, health, housing, and community infrastructure, a host of other agencies facilitate the coordination between different agencies at the national level and between national and local levels, and are critical for sustaining resilience outcomes (see table on page 68).

---

98   World Bank. 2015. *More and Better Spending: Connecting People to Improved Water Supply and Sanitation in Indonesia.* Water Supply and Sanitation Public Expenditure Review (WSS-PER). Washington, DC.

Working together. In one Cirebon City neighborhood, residents formed a mangrove working group and partnered with the Department of Environment and Forestry (DLH) to plant 3,000 mangrove trees to prevent coastal erosion and protect and support livelihoods.

Institutional Responsibilities Related to Building Resilience of the Urban Poor

Departments/ Agencies	Central Responsibilities	Relevance to Building Resilience of the Urban Poor
Ministry of National Development Planning/ National Development Planning Agency (BAPPENAS)	Ensuring that national development goals are met through required budgeting, planning, and regulation. Developing the long-term development plan (RPJPN), medium-term development plan (RPJMN) and Annual Government Work Plan (RKP). Prepare national development policies related to climate change, such as the Climate Resilience Development Policy (CRDP/PBI) and Low Carbon Development Initiatives (LCDI/PRK) Planning the development of infrastructure, particularly water resources, transportation, public housing, sanitation, drinking water services, and other basic infrastructure needs. Ensuring the quality of construction by improving the quality of human resources and enforcing construction in the field.	Given its powerful planning function, and as a cross-sectoral and regional coordinator, it is well placed to mainstream urban resilience across tiers of government. Manage the Indonesia Climate Change Trust Fund. Can help engender greater collaboration across scales of government and between different sectoral ministries and agencies essential for resilience. Influential in defining the development agenda/ priorities and implementing international agendas that have a bearing on the resilience of the urban poor (e.g., the New Urban Agenda, Sustainable Development Goals, Paris Agreement, and Sendai Framework for Disaster Risk Reduction). Potential for ensuring that the resilience of the urban poor receives greater prominence in future iterations of climate change policies and plans. Has a role in integrating water resource management, particularly planning and implementing flood risk protection for the urban poor in most affected watershed locations.
Ministry of Finance	Formulating, stipulating, and implementing policies in terms of budgeting, taxes, customs and excise, treasury, state assets management, fiscal balance, and budget financing and risk management.	Under the Fiscal Policy Agency, set up the Centre for Climate Change Financing Policy to advance integration of climate considerations in fiscal decision-making. National Designated Authority/focal point for the Green Climate Fund.
Ministry of Home Affairs	Developing the participatory planning and budgeting process (Musrenbang), which informs the Annual Budget Plan (APBD) that has an important bearing on major domestic development programs. Ensuring stable governance and improving public services.	Lead agency for undertaking Musrenbang that informs the APBD; can be leveraged to channel funding to underresourced district governments and toward programming that builds the resilience of the urban poor. Had a role in the design and delivery of anti-poverty programs in collaboration with other agencies/ministries giving it the ability to mainstream resilience of the urban poor in future anti-poverty programs.
Ministry of Agrarian Affairs and Spatial Planning	Developing spatial (RTRW) and spatial detailed plans (RDTR). Formulating, stipulating, and implementing policies related to spatial planning and land infrastructure, management and use.[a]	Its influence on spatial planning processes gives it considerable power to ensure that the urban poor are not made to reside on exposed land, through the promotion of inclusive land planning and zoning practices. Has a crucial role in discharging the central government's commitment to integrated land management and administration,[a] and therefore can integrate vulnerabilities of the urban poor within these processes.

Departments/ Agencies	Central Responsibilities	Relevance to Building Resilience of the Urban Poor
Ministry of Environment and Forestry	Overseeing national environmental protection and management, including climate change control based on Law No. 32/2009 and Presidential Regulation No. 92/2020, (as major role and national coordinator for climate change issues). According to the mandate of Law No. 32/2009 on Environment Protection and Management, dealing with planning, utilization, control, maintenance, supervision, and law enforcement related to environment protection and management, including climate change (Article 4). According to Law No. 32/2009 (Articles 10 and 16), the preparation of environmental protection and management plans (RPPLH) and Strategic Environmental Assessment (KLHS) should consist of a climate change adaptation plan as one mandatory requirement, including the levels of climate vulnerability and adaptive capacity. It would be an opportunity to mainstream issues related to the climate risk of the urban poor. Article 5 of Presidential Regulation No. 92/2020 on Ministry of Environment and Forestry states that the ministry carries out the functions for formulating, stipulating, coordinating, and synchronizing the implementation of policies of climate change control. To carry out these functions, the Minister appoints the Director General of Climate Change as the person responsible for overall functions related to climate change, such as formulating, implementing, and preparing the norms, standards, procedures and criteria, coordination, and synchronization, as well as providing technical guidance and supervision and also evaluating and reporting on programs and activities related to climate change control (Articles 29 and 30). Directorate General of Climate Change also designated as National Focal Point for United Nations Framework Convention on Climate Change in Indonesia.	Charged with overseeing environmental impact assessment processes provides it with an important opportunity to mainstream issues of climate vulnerability of the urban poor within the guidelines for these. National Designated Authority/focal point for the Adaptation Fund.
National Agency for Disaster Management	Coordinating all disaster management activities in Indonesia. Incorporating the Sendai Framework for Disaster Risk Reduction into Indonesia's national development strategies. Implementing the country's 15-year road map (2015–2030) for creating more people-centered disaster risk reduction.	Disaster risk management planning can be used as an effective entry point for enhancing the resilience of the urban poor through a specific focus on their particular vulnerabilities and exposure to shocks and stresses.

Departments/ Agencies	Central Responsibilities	Relevance to Building Resilience of the Urban Poor
National Team for Acceleration of Poverty Reduction (TNP2K)	Multi-stakeholder, cross-agency group charged with improving the implementation of poverty reduction programs. Mandated to establish and improve a targeting system for social assistance programs.	Developing poverty reduction policies and programs, synergizing these with agencies and ministries, and supervising their implementation puts it in a strong position to advance the resilience of both the rural and urban poor.
National Coordination Team for the Achievement of the Sustainable Development Goals	High-powered multi-stakeholder group charged with four components: (i) social development, (ii) economic development, (iii) environment development, and (iv) justice and governance.	Backed by presidential decrees, the team can play a vitally important role in mainstreaming the vulnerabilities of the urban poor in sustainable development policies. Many current interventions already focus on the urban poor, and therefore the inclusion of resilience within these is a logical next step.

a   Devex. Ministry of Agrarian Affairs and Spatial Planning/National Land Agency (ATR/BPN).
Source: Government websites and consultants for the Asian Development Bank

Cross-boundary and cross-sectoral cooperation needs to be strengthened with an explicit purpose of building resilience. The existing frameworks of decentralized governance in Indonesia provide a solid basis for local action that highlights local needs. However, enhanced coordination is needed at all levels with an explicit focus on resilience, especially since natural hazards do not follow administrative boundaries and may have impacts that cross administrative boundaries; and exposure to hazards may be a result of actions taken elsewhere beyond a particular administrative boundary (e.g., dumping of waste in rivers can lead to flooding in downstream neighborhoods). Interlocal groupings (whether formal "metropolitan areas" or less formal arrangements) allow for transboundary planning and solutions to entire city regions and can be critical for addressing the cross-boundary issues of climate and disaster risk (including issues related to water, agriculture, and marine and coastal) that affect the urban poor. Similarly, collaboration among institutions will help to enable complementarity and synergies in the activities led by different agencies and will also help to avoid duplication. The existing institutional architecture should give sufficient importance to this much-needed resilience coordination role across levels and departments. One approach could be to enable an existing institution to act as a coordinating body and to perform tasks related to (i) coordinating mandates across scales between national and local institutions and within urban areas—to identify existing programs that contribute to building resilience of the urban poor and ensure that these are harmonized and complementary; (ii) enabling the coordination of activities between districts, particularly in situations where risk and resilience cross local geographic and administrative boundaries; (iii) identifying poverty, socioeconomic, and climate and disaster risk data needs and coordinating and facilitating data accessibility to inform projects and programs; (iv) coordinating with the private sector to engage in resilience-building; and (v) incorporating perspectives and priorities from the urban poor, both directly and through partnership with CSOs and NGOs.

Capacity of local governments on climate-responsive local development planning and management should be enhanced. This requires making available climate risk information at different local government levels and improving capacities to use and apply such information in preparing development plans and informing decisions for policies and investments. Programs, projects, and activities identified using climate risk information will be prioritized and consolidated in investment programs, which get funded during the budgeting process, subject to the resource envelope for a particular year. Those aligned with existing climate resilience development policies and included in regional development plans are more likely to secure budget allocation. Intergovernmental fiscal transfers are critical to complement locally generated revenues. However, the fiscal transfer mechanism needs to be simplified to facilitate the transfer of money for implementing the priority programs, activities, and projects. Public–private partnerships can be fostered to leverage private sector resources for urban infrastructure construction. Part of capacity-building for local governments is raising the awareness and understanding of local governments on current and future climate and disaster risk, and this should be done whenever there is a change in local government leadership. This can facilitate recognition and buy-in of the importance of building resilience of the urban poor.

The power of civil society organizations can be harnessed to enhance the resilience of the urban poor. It would be useful to create a platform connecting government budget makers with eligible non-state providers. This will allow government agencies to be more aware of many CSOs and their capacities. At the same time, it will help CSOs increase their awareness on government programs and explore collaboration with government ministries. It might entail building the capacity and systems within government to solicit and evaluate proposals from CSOs to build resilience. It could also require upgrading the ability of CSOs to furnish the right documents and information to ensure compliance with government procedures. Finally, it is crucial to enhance trust between government and civil society by including CSOs in government committees and stakeholder groups to ensure the gradual growth of cooperation through regular engagement.

Climate, Disaster Risk, and Poverty Data in Support of Resilience

Appropriate and reliable data on climate and disaster risk, and poverty are an essential enabling factor for building resilience of the urban poor. The multidimensional nature of poverty, the range of current and future hazards, and their potential direct and indirect impacts on assets, livelihoods, and well-being of the urban poor need to be considered when planning, designing, and implementing poverty reduction programs in order to build resilience. Particularly important is analysis that allows an understanding of the spatial and temporal distribution of hazards, exposure, and vulnerabilities, across a range of scales (from households, communities, and settlements to cities and urban regions). Both technology and community-generated information play a significant role—with analysis that brings these together being particularly important.

Integrating poverty and climate and disaster risk data is particularly important for targeting interventions that build the resilience of the urban poor. Not all the urban poor live in locations that are exposed to climate-related and other hazards, and the people living in the most exposed locations may not be the poorest urban residents. Risk mapping is an important approach for understanding these overlaps. At the city or municipal level, for example, a map showing the areas that are more prone to flooding (indicating the "hazard") can be overlaid with maps that show population density (describing "exposure") and poverty incidence (as a key indicator of "vulnerability"). The product of these elements would be maps identifying the most vulnerable neighborhoods. This type of data can help prioritize resilience interventions. For instance, not all populations that are exposed will have the same amount of vulnerability to a particular hazard. Therefore, combining information on exposure and vulnerability will provide a clear insight into people who are most at risk in a particular area. Furthermore, a combination of data will enhance an understanding of each component of risk. For example, a more complete picture of vulnerability can emerge from combining different datasets on health, education, financial services, and social capital.

Data should be produced both by poor urban communities (through surveys and participatory approaches) and by modern technologies (through sensors, satellites, ICT, etc.). Data on hazards are collected through Satellite Remote Sensing (SRS) (e.g., to spot and track cyclones), weather forecasts (that rely on ground instruments, balloons, or satellites), climate models (that combine data on future greenhouse gas emissions with a range of other environmental variables from different sources to project changes in key climate parameters), or household surveys. Data on exposure are collected through SRS and GIS technologies (e.g., to gauge settlements or population clusters that may lie in the path of cyclones), census data, or participatory methods (e.g., maps, transect walks, and shared learning dialogues). Data on vulnerability can be collected through SRS (e.g., where the quality of roof materials of a house can portend the socioeconomic status of its inhabitants that is correlated with their vulnerability), combining data points from existing surveys on health, education, and financial services, or through

participatory exercises (e.g., participatory vulnerability assessments).

Indonesia already has a number of sources from which these data can be collated and analyzed. With regard to vulnerability, a number of existing surveys and datasets in the country can provide data points:

- Key surveys: The Demographic and Health Survey provides data on a number of variables that have a bearing on vulnerability such as access to water and sanitation, household wealth, basic education, employment, access to insurance, health status, and gender empowerment.[99]

- Similarly, the Indonesia Family Life Survey[100] provides longitudinal data on a number of crucial variables that have a bearing on vulnerability including community support and social capital, migration, educational achievement, financial status, and health status. Much of these data are disaggregated for urban and rural areas.

- Financial services and inclusion indices: Institutions such as the World Bank collect and distribute data on financial services and inclusion such as depth of savings, access to credit, and dependency on remittances, all of which have a bearing on vulnerability.

In terms of exposure data, certain existing sets and sources of data can be used to calculate the degree to which the urban poor in Indonesia are exposed to the impacts of climate change. These include but are not limited to

---

[99] National Population and Family Planning Board (BKKBN), Statistics Indonesia (BPS), Ministry of Health (Kemenkes), and ICF. 2018. *Indonesia Demographic and Health Survey 2017.* Jakarta.

[100] J. Strauss, F. Witoelar, B. Sikoki, and A.M. Wattie. 2009. *The Fourth Wave of the Indonesia Family Life Survey (IFLS4): Overview and Field Report.* April. WR-675/1-NIA/NICHD.

Considering local context in project designs. Data from the community are used to develop detailed engineering designs for projects in informal settlements to ensure that these take into consideration local conditions, including disaster and climate risks.

- The Demographic and Health Survey (footnote 99): This provides data on a number of variables that a bearing on resilience such as construction materials of floor, roof, and outer walls of the house.

- SRS data: A set of existing web applications can be used to access high-resolution SRS data on exposure for different parts of the world. For instance, a decreasing Normalized Difference Vegetation Index[101] can be indicative of increasing exposure to a range of hazards including drought. This is made available by the United States National Aeronautics and Space Administration (NASA) through a range of easily accessible channels.[102]

- Existing exposure maps and atlases: Communities of practice working to ameliorate the risk of diverse shocks and stresses have prepared a plethora of exposure maps and atlases to better understand exposure. For instance, the World Food Programme's Food Security and Vulnerability Atlas for Indonesia provides district-level data on a range of indicators including the degree to which populations are exposed to potential food security shocks (spanning availability as well as access).[103]

For hazards, the country has a number of existing sources of data on the hazards with likely impacts. These include but are not limited to:

- Climate change projections and scenarios: A number of different organizations have

[101] A.J. Peters, E. Walter-Shea, L. Ji, A. Viña, M. Hayes, and M. Svoboda. 2002. Drought Monitoring with NDVI-based Standardized Vegetation Index. *Photogrammetric Engineering and Remote Sensing.* 68. pp. 71–75.
[102] National Aeronautics and Space Administration (NASA) Moderate Resolution Imaging Spectroradiometer (MODIS). MODIS Vegetation Index Products (NDVI and EVI).
[103] World Food Programme. 2015. *Indonesia – Food Security and Vulnerability Atlas, 2015.*

produced various types of downscaled projections for Indonesia that can be used to gauge hydrometeorological hazards in the country. A few notable examples include downscaled models outputs (60 km resolution) by the Australian Department of Foreign Affairs and Trade and CSIRO,[104] country-specific projections on the World Bank's Climate Change Knowledge Portal (CCKP),[105] and downscaling done by academic research units in universities (e.g., Nottingham and Norwich).[106]

- Impact models: A number of initiatives have employed climate change projections to model impacts that the changing climate will have on different sectors. These include the International Food Policy Research Institute on the economy[107] and IPB University on the water sector, among others.[108]

- Existing hazard maps: A range of hazard maps exist for Indonesia that delineate the kinds of hazards that different parts of the country might face. For instance, the Geospatial Information Agency (formerly known as National Coordinating Agency for Surveys and Mapping) provides maps on flooding and landslides,[109] and the Agency of Meteorology, Climatology and Geophysics has a large number of maps for a variety of hazards (including specific maps for urban areas).[110]

Two databases deserve special mention in the context of climate and disaster risk information. First, SIDIK (Sistem Informasi dan Data Indeks Kerentanan) Climate Change is a data and information platform on climate change vulnerability, covering all areas in Indonesia, including urban areas. It provides data and information at village, city and district, and provincial levels based on socioeconomic, demographic, geographic, environmental, and infrastructure data derived from the Village Potential Data (PODES - Potensi Desa) and also extreme rainfall data from the Meteorology, Climatology, and Geophysical Agency (BMKG). The platform provides vulnerability maps for climate change risk, drought risk, and flood risk. It also provides spider graphs for Adaptive Capacity Index (IKA) and Exposure and Sensitivity Index (IKS). The indicators for IKS include the number of households living in riverbanks, buildings on riverbank, drinking water sources, poverty, and income sources. The indicators for IKA include electricity, education, health facilities, and road infrastructure. A higher IKS value represents higher vulnerability, and a higher IKA represents higher adaptive capacity. SIDIK was established for adaptation-related policies and projects. The platform also provides features for regional authorities to add or remove indicators used in calculations and projections. The platform is managed by the Directorate of Climate Change Adaptation, Ministry of Environment and Forestry, the Center for Climate Risk and Opportunity Management in Southeast Asia Pacific, Bogor Institute of Agriculture, and BPS (Statistics Indonesia). Data provided by SIDIK can also be accessed by the general public, thereby increasing awareness on climate change. However, the current

[104] J.L. McGregor, K.C. Nguyen, D.G.C. Kirono, and J.J. Katzfey. 2016. High-Resolution Climate Projections for the Islands of Lombok and Sumbawa, Nusa Tenggara Barat Province, Indonesia: Challenges and Implications. *Climate Risk Management.* 12. pp. 32–44.

[105] World Bank. 2011. *Vulnerability, Risk Reduction, and Adaptation to Climate Change: Indonesia.* Climate Risk and Adaptation Country Profile.

[106] M. Hulme and N. Sheard. 1999. *Climate Change Scenarios for Indonesia.* Norwich, UK: Climatic Research Unit.

[107] R. Oktaviani, S. Amaliah, C. Ringler, M.W. Rosegrant, and T.B. Sulser. 2011. The Impact of Global Climate Change on the Indonesian Economy. *IFPRI Discussion Paper* 1148. Washington, DC: International Food Policy Research Institute.

[108] H. Pawitan. 2018. Climate Change Impacts on Availability and Vulnerability of Indonesia Water Resources. *IOP Conference Series: Earth and Environmental Science.* 200 (1):012003.

[109] The Geospatial Information Agency was created to coordinate the development of geospatial information in Indonesia. See Ina-geoportal.

[110] World Bank, United Nations Office for Disaster Risk Reduction, National Hydrological and Meteorological Services, World Meteorological Organization, and Global Facility for Disaster Reduction and Recovery. 2013. *Country Assessment Report for Indonesia: Strengthening of Hydrometeorological Services in Southeast Asia.*

data are based on analyses undertaken in 2011, 2014, and 2018 and need to be updated regularly.

Second, InaRISK is a disaster risk assessment portal. It uses the ArcGIS server to present the spatial distribution of disaster risk for the entire Indonesian archipelago. The Disaster Risk Index is determined by combining the hazard, vulnerability, and capacity index values according to Perka BNPB 2/2012. InaRISK provides maps with scales ranging 1:250,000, 1:50,000, and 1:25,000, which allow users to zoom in and out of regional, city, or district boundaries within Indonesia. It also provides IRBI (Indeks Risiko Bencana Indonesia), which is a disaster tier index rating the level of disaster risk for each district or city in Indonesia. Information from InaRISK can be used for spatial planning and selection of disaster risk reduction measures. For urban areas, it can provide information on hazard maps, vulnerability maps, and risk maps. The limitation of this platform itself lies in the data coverage of only 136 out of total 514 districts and cities in Indonesia.

A range of specific interventions could contribute to better climate and poverty data that support building resilience of the urban poor.

Package available information for specific sectors with a role in enhancing resilience of the urban poor. The implications of downscaled climate data for sectors such as water, marine and coastal, and health in urban areas should be made available as an easy reference guide for decision-making when developing new programs and initiatives.

Ensure information sharing across administrative boundaries and strengthening compatibility between data systems. This means that information that currently is primarily accessible and used within one administrative unit (either geographical or departmental) can be used to support activities by other units as needed. Where memorandums of understanding are required to access data, the process should be clear and straightforward, with appropriate capacity support to agencies that may not have prior experience of these.

Identify a single entity with primary responsibility for collating and distributing climate risk data for enhancing the resilience of the urban poor. A plethora of organizations are producing and/or distributing data on climate change with implications for enhancing the resilience of the urban poor. This increases the transaction costs of employing and analyzing these data. Instead, the government should nominate a single entity or organization from within or outside government (e.g., within the University of Indonesia) to lead data collation and distribution.

Communicate risk data to the urban poor. Apart from ensuring that data are packaged for informing programs and policies and distributed to technocrats and experts, the information should also be communicated to the urban poor. While certain kinds of early warning and disaster preparedness data are communicated to vulnerable populations, data on a broader number of variables that influence risk (e.g., sanitation or changes in quality and quantity of groundwater) should also be distributed to the urban poor in accessible formats to influence individual decision-making.

Consider new initiatives on the use of novel ICT-based approaches for generating risk data for the urban poor. Indonesia has a high and rapidly expanding rate of smartphone usage. This should be leveraged by expanding partnerships with entities such as the UN Global Pulse (the United Nations Secretary-General's initiative on big data for development) that already has an active laboratory in Indonesia to develop risk data at scale for the urban poor using cell phones and other technologies.

Securing Finance for Building Resilience of the Urban Poor

Building resilience of the urban poor will require additional and refocused financing. Financing for resilience of the urban poor needs to be identified, stimulated, secured, and sustained for impact, both in individual interventions and also across an ecosystem of urban financing related to resilience and wider poverty reduction. First, financing for resilience has to come from a combination of sources, including standard fiscal balance transfers made to local government, climate change-related domestic funding sources established by the government, external grants from bilateral agencies and CSOs, and global climate funds. Allocation of such resources should be based on a robust understanding of current and future climate risk and the pathways for resilience. Second, recognizing the importance of building resilience at all scales, such funding should be delivered by a range of appropriate institutions at appropriate volume, subsidiarity, and scale. Some of this finance will need to directly reach low-income households in order to contribute to building resilient livelihoods and assets (including housing); some also needs to reach organized community groups as a means of strengthening community infrastructure in partnerships with local governments. Similarly, finances that are generated by municipal governments and/or allocated to municipalities will be most effective if these have the appropriate political will and technical capacity to use these funds in building resilience of the urban poor. Third, financing mechanisms also need to bridge different scales—for example, linking community drainage (which can largely be implemented by community members) with trunk infrastructure (which requires larger investment and more advanced technical skills). Fourth, systems should be in place to track such finance to ensure funds are spent appropriately (on necessary activities) and effectively (achieving value for money). This will require close working relationships between local governments and urban poor and community-level groups in low-income urban neighborhoods. Low-income urban communities with established savings groups often have higher levels of financial literacy and may already have collective financial management structures in place.

Standard fiscal balance transfers have the potential to advance the common objective of poverty reduction and climate resilience. Provinces, districts, and municipalities in Indonesia (with the exception of Aceh, Papua, West Papua, and Yogyakarta) receive three categories of fiscal balance transfers: General Allocation (DAU), Special Allocation (DAK), and Revenue Sharing (DBH). The DAK has specific targets or indicators set by the national government but must be delivered by the local governments. Health, education, and poverty reduction are continuously included in the requirements for DAK spending, and thus, if informed by climate risk considerations, have the potential to reduce vulnerability to climate impacts. The DAK is divided into two categories: physical and non-physical spending. The physical spending usually funds infrastructure, while the non-physical is aimed at funding activities that relate to processes, such as trainings, townhall meetings, and other community empowerment programs. Both physical (e.g., resilient community infrastructure) and non-physical (e.g., capacity-building of local government communities to maintain resilient infrastructure) interventions are critical for advancing the resilience of the urban poor. In addition, the Village Fund (Dana Desa) funds development activities based on priorities identified by the village head and village council. The Ministry of Environment and Forestry has prepared guidelines for the use of village funds for climate change-related activities, which include use for building activities and infrastructure for climate change adaptation and mitigation, such as harvesting rainwater and preventing floods, drought, and landslides. This is an important modality that can be utilized by vulnerable groups, including the urban poor through the communities to build their climate resilience.

The Kelurahan Fund can be strategically utilized to advance resilience in the context of wider local development. In addition to the standard fiscal transfers, district governments and municipalities receive additional General Allocation (DAU) funds in the form of the Kelurahan Fund targeted for development in the kelurahans or villages in municipalities. The fund has two priorities. The first is to fund the construction and maintenance of education, health, and housing infrastructure. The second is to fund community empowerment activities such as trainings, village-level enterprises, and village meetings. The Kelurahan Fund provides a new opportunity for villages in municipalities to have additional fund to finance climate resilience-related activities. The value of the fund is not as big as the Village Fund, but, if utilized wisely, could contribute significantly to climate change targets in municipalities. For example, with appropriate understanding of climate risk among local governments, the Kelurahan Fund can be used to strategically finance infrastructure that

has the primary purpose of resilience-building, introduce nature-based solutions, improve waste management activities that have a direct bearing on resilience, and build the capacity of local communities on disaster preparedness. It is also important to explore the potential of funding social protection measures using the Kelurahan Fund in order to deal with shocks. In the aftermath of COVID-19, similar efforts were made through the Village Fund, to reallocate a portion of the fund typically used for village infrastructure to provide unconditional cash transfers to residents affected by the crisis but not eligible under any other assistance programs. A shortcoming of the Kelurahan Fund is that the planning for its utilization is determined by the district government or municipalities, unlike the Village Fund, for which the utilization of the budget is determined by the villagers led by the village head and the village council–Badan Permusyawaratan Desa (BPD).

Long-term technical support is needed to integrate adaptation priorities in local budget. To finance climate resilience activities from their local budgets, local governments must integrate targets and plans for climate resilience activities into regional development planning documents (RPJMD and RKPD). This is the basis for ensuring that the allocation of funding for climate change is included in the Regional Revenues and Expenditures Budget (APBD). This document

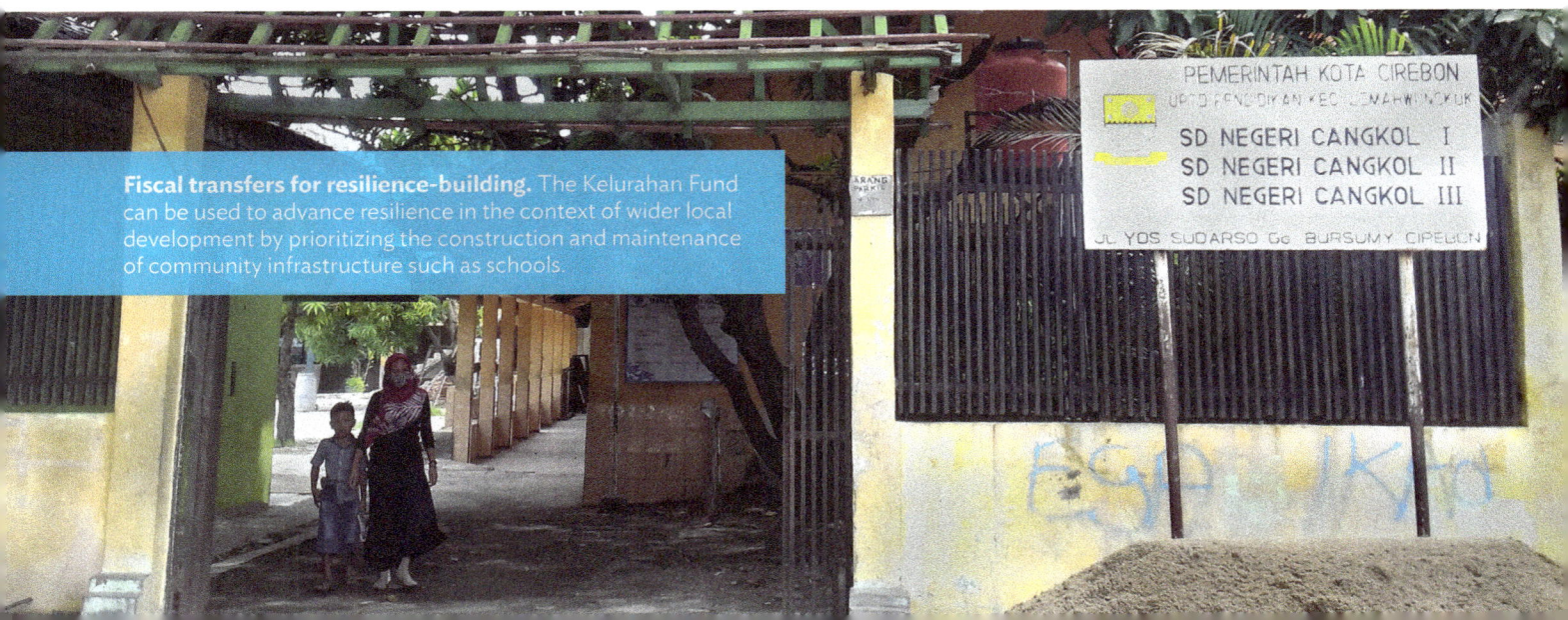

Fiscal transfers for resilience-building. The Kelurahan Fund can be used to advance resilience in the context of wider local development by prioritizing the construction and maintenance of community infrastructure such as schools.

then needs to be adopted into provincial, district, or city regulations. Most local governments, even at the provincial level, need technical support to mainstream climate resilience development into local development planning. National government agencies, in particular BAPPENAS, in cooperation with donor agencies and NGOs, have provided technical support to assist local governments on climate-responsive planning and budgeting. To ensure the implementation and achievement of the RPJMD targets, it must be ensured that the budget allocation is included in the APBD. Once the APBD is adopted into a local regulation, the local government can allocate a budget from their revenues, both from fiscal transfers and locally generated revenue. However, even after completing the document, the political process to integrate the climate change targets into the local budget and for it to finally pass as a local regulation can be challenging. A new initiative called Lingkar Temu Kabupaten Lestari–LTKL (Association for District Governments for Sustainability) was recently set up to form an association of district governments with strong commitments to address climate change mitigation and adaptation. With the association's secretariat assistance, district governments have initiated integrating their climate change targets into their local budget process—and some have even completed doing so. Local governments with strong commitments to address climate change mitigation and adaptation such as members of the LTKL could be at the forefront of a new breed of local governments that seize the initiative to utilize public or international funding for their respective climate change targets. A strong directive is needed from the National Budget Law (APBN) on climate change targets in order to mainstream public funding for climate change mitigation and adaptation in public budgets at national and local levels.

The scope of the Regional Incentives Fund can be expanded to explicitly incentivize adaptation. In 2011, the government created a new incentives fund called the Regional Incentives

Fund, or DID, as a new fiscal transfer scheme to local governments. The DID serves as a performance-based grant that incentivizes local governments based on achievement of specific indicators along financial management, basic service delivery, and poverty reduction. For 2020, the government added a new requirement for waste management to reduce plastic use. Theoretically, the national government could introduce other climate change-related conditions for the transfer of DID to local governments. By imposing climate change requirements, the local governments can avoid political wrangling for the budget and receive DID if they implement climate change-related targets.

Climate change targets can be promoted in the budget for special autonomous regions. The Special Autonomy Fund is transferred to three provinces: Aceh, Papua, and West Papua. This fund was established as part of the Special Autonomy Law for the three provinces to compensate for decades of separatist conflict and to accelerate their development. The national government earmarked 2% of the national revenue to finance the Special Autonomy Fund for Papua and West Papua for 20 years until 2022. For Aceh, the national government earmarked 2% of its revenue to fund the Aceh Autonomy Fund for the first 15 years and 1% for the remaining 5 years until 2027. Between 2002 and 2018, the two provinces (including West Papua) received Rp142.5 trillion ($8.8 billion). Yogyakarta receives the Special Fund for Yogyakarta at an amount determined by both the national and Yogyakarta governments on an annual basis. All four provinces have relatively greater discretion to utilize the Special (Autonomy) Funds. Districts and *Kelurahan* in these provinces receive the fund transfers through the provincial governments. NGOs and development projects tend to focus more on the Special Autonomy Provinces of Aceh, Papua, and West Papua. Given their special autonomy statuses, these provincial governments can take initiative to prioritize climate change targets in the provincial budget. The Papua Special Autonomy Law also provided a strong basis for environmental targets. Therefore, lobbying these provincial governments to integrate climate change targets into their budgets is less complicated than in provinces with regular autonomy status.

Climate finance offers significant potential to unlock wider financing for building resilience of the poor. Climate finance is generally understood as a resource mobilized to fund actions that mitigate or adapt to climate change. While climate finance can be critical for building resilience of urban poor, the following constraints should be recognized. First, it is generally agreed that the quantity of climate finance available is not commensurate to the level of need,[111] thus requiring a strategic approach on its usage. Second, a large percentage of available climate finance usually goes to mitigation. This trend is apparent in Indonesia too where the budget for RAN-GRK was far larger than the one for the National Action Plan for Climate Change Adaptation (Rancana Aksi National–Perubahan Iklim or RAN–API, the predecessor of PBI 2020–2045).[112] Also, sectors crucial for mitigation such as forestry, transport, waste, and energy have received the lion's share of climate finance in the country. In the case of adaptation, the focus has been largely on rural adaptation to assist farmers or fishers to better improve their adaptability to the changing weather conditions. Third, the significant overlap between "development" and "adaptation needs" further creates confusion in allocating climate finance for adaptation. Thus, climate finance for building resilience of the urban poor should be strategically used to unlock the potential for poverty reduction programs and wider development programs to deliver on resilience and to de-risk other forms of financing for resilience. For example, a small amount of public climate finance could act as

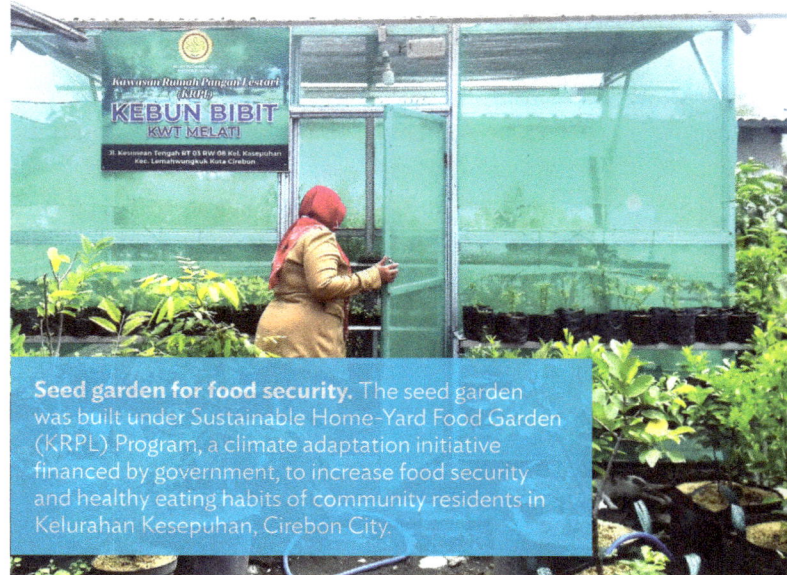

Seed garden for food security. The seed garden was built under Sustainable Home-Yard Food Garden (KRPL) Program, a climate adaptation initiative financed by government, to increase food security and healthy eating habits of community residents in Kelurahan Kesepuhan, Cirebon City.

collateral for private sector micro loans given to residents of informal settlements to improve the structural integrity of their houses. Similarly, climate finance could be used for subsidizing the premiums of the urban poor (e.g., street vendors) for hazard indexed weather insurance that can be provided by the private sector.[113]

Climate finance allocated to national government agencies can be used strategically to support resilience-building of the urban poor. Sources of climate finance in Indonesia include the central government, local governments, international development partners, and bespoke funds. By far, the largest contributor of these is the central government that provides over two-thirds of the total climate finance in the country through the state budget.[114] National government line agencies receive the vast majority of climate finance and make some allocations to local governments to execute measures locally. Recognizing the important role central government agencies in the design of large-scale poverty reduction programs, it will be critical that climate finance is used to improve the design and delivery of such programs, and,

[111] J. Keenan, E. Chu, and J. Peterson. 2019. From Funding to Financing: Perspectives Shaping a Research Agenda for Investment in Urban Climate Adaptation. *International Journal of Urban Sustainable Development.* 11 (3). pp. 297–308.

[112] H. Imelda, T. Kuswardono, and F. Tumiwa. 2017. *Climate Change Financing for Cities in Indonesia. Case Study: Kupang.* Jakarta: Institute for Essential Services Reform.

[113] R. Patel, G. Walker, M. Bhatt, and V. Pathak. 2017. The Demand for Disaster Microinsurance for Small Businesses in Urban Slums: The Results of Surveys in Three Indian Cities. *PLOS Currents Disasters.* Mar 1 . Edition 1.

[114] Climate Policy Initiative and Ministry of Finance. 2014. *The Landscape of Public Climate Finance in Indonesia.*

where appropriate, finance outputs that contribute to transformational adaptation at the local level or help strengthen systems that would allow further adaptation actions to flow. The national government can also help local governments to access climate finance to overcome barriers to invest in resilience, such as through innovative land use management tools (e.g., land value capture) that would allow local governments to generate revenue for building resilience of the urban poor.

Local government capacity should be enhanced to access and manage climate finance. The demand for climate change funding is rising at the local level (partly due to the preparation of subnational climate plans). However, local governments currently access and manage a fraction of the climate finance in the country. By some estimates, this is disproportionately spent on indirect mitigation activities such as forestry.[115] Moving forward, climate finance should increasingly support local governments to increase awareness of climate impacts, improve the capacity for risk-informed decision-making, develop adaptation plans and strategies, and involve grassroots organizations in resilience-building processes. Moreover, international climate finance is still considered to be out of reach by local governments given the complicated requirements. These international financing schemes need to conduct better outreach programs to invite local governments to take advantage of the funds.

It is necessary to identify groups and organizations with the ability to use climate finance for the urban poor. At times, non-traditional actors could provide a more effective conduit for channeling resources for enhancing the resilience of the urban poor, and the regulatory environment needs to be structured to permit them to access and manage climate

finance. This could include CSOs such as slum and shack dwellers federations that have experience managing finances (e.g., from community savings groups). They have community-level structures and institutions to involve the poor and vulnerable in decision-making and may already have collective financial management structures in place that can enable them to be effective partners and implementing agents for funded projects.

Indonesia has made strides in climate finance readiness, but some institutional gaps need to be further strengthened. Readiness is understood to be "...the capacities of countries to plan for, access, deliver, and monitor and report on climate finance, both international and domestic, in ways that are catalytic and fully integrated with national development priorities" (footnote 115). The country has made strides in strengthening institutional mechanisms, policy instruments, and the finance architecture, but there is scope to enhance multilevel planning, programming, and coordination; improving resource flows to the local level and engaging the private sector to a greater degree (footnote 112). To organize the financing for climate change, the government set up the Centre for Climate Change Financing Policy (Pusat Kebijakan Pendanaan Perubahan Iklim dan Multilateral, or PKPPIM) under the Fiscal Policy Agency at the Ministry of Finance. However, the center currently has a large focus on mitigation, especially on renewable energy. Improved institutional coordination is also needed to facilitate interaction with different climate funds. For example, the Ministry of Finance is the National Designated Authority or focal point for the Green Climate Fund, the Ministry of Environment and Forestry is the National Designated Authority for the Adaptation Fund, and the Indonesia Climate Change Trust Fund (ICCTF) is managed by BAPPENAS.

---

[115] V. Vandeweerd, Y. Glemarec, and S. Billett. 2012. *Readiness for Transformative Climate Finance: A Framework for Understanding What It Means to Be Ready to Use Climate Finance.* New York: United Nations Development Programme.

Strategic Investments to Scale Up Resilience-Building of the Urban Poor

A drainage channel by an elementary school and playground in Cangkol Utara, Kelurahan Lemahwungkuk, Cirebon City. Well-functioning drainage plays a critical role to deal with the impacts of increased precipitation due to climate change.

Indonesia has a wide set of poverty reduction programs across different sectors that support the urban poor in human development and infrastructure-related needs. These programs provide a good foundation for building resilience of the urban poor to climate-related shocks and stresses. Some of these programs with certain degree of adjustments can help the urban poor better cope with climate risks, and in some cases even incrementally adapt to the changes in climate. However, given the scale of climate risk the country faces, for these programs to facilitate transformational adaptation, additional climate investments in key strategic areas are needed that take a more cross-cutting and integrated approach. These areas can provide the support structure for local governments, communities, and households to invest in long-term risk management and thereby help catalyze further investments needed to achieve wider transformational change. Based on analyses presented in the previous chapters, this chapter recommends five key strategic areas for climate investments. These topics are aligned with the priorities of the RPJMN 2020–2024 and PBI 2020–2045.

Investing in Strengthening Awareness on Future Climate Risk for Urban Poverty Reduction

Understanding future climate risk in priority sectors and its impact on the urban poor. Climate change, both discrete climate events and risk related to long-term changes such as slow onset events, may continue to change the conditions under which poverty reduction programs operate. Thus, it is critical to factor thinking on long-term risk for strengthening resilience of the urban poor. This risk may seem remote, however, and thereby not considering it in policy, plans, and programs may risk locking in future impacts that may be detrimental to the objectives of poverty reduction. For example, decisions on spatial planning may ignore longer-term increase in temperature and promote certain urban forms that could increase the exposure of urban informal workers to heat stress and associated respiratory diseases. PBI 2020–2045 has identified four priority sectors for climate change adaptation: marine and coastal, water, agriculture, and health. Since all these sectors can directly or indirectly impact the lives and livelihoods of the urban poor, a thorough understanding of how current and future climate risk in such sectors interact or will interact with the lives, livelihoods, and well-being of the urban poor is critical for the design of current poverty reduction policies and programs in order to ensure such programs promote the transformational change needed to reduce poverty and strengthen resilience. This would require strengthening awareness among decision-makers, technocrats, local government, utilities, MSMEs, financial institutions, and communities on long-term climate risk.

Understanding future climate risk to inform current plans and programs. A good starting point is to have a comprehensive understanding of the full spectrum of plausible impacts of climate change—the range of what might happen over time—on human development, infrastructure, and the environment of the urban poor, which forms the basis of all poverty reduction programs. This will help improve, refocus, and introduce new elements in such programs. For example, understanding the long-term impact of climate change on food production can inform the need for diversifying food staples being provided through social assistance programs. Similarly, for programs promoting access to clean water for urban communities, it becomes critical to understand the longer-term reliability of specific water sources due to changing climate, such as groundwater in coastal areas, and accordingly introduce integrated water management systems. Most importantly, understanding such plausible impacts may encourage prioritizing *ex ante* actions to reduce vulnerabilities rather than *ex post*, when accompanied with suitable incentives.

Understanding climate risk at systems level to identify cross-sector and multiscale solutions. This needs to be strengthened at a wider systems level and not just at a specific project level, in order to ensure the proposed resilience-building interventions are able to address the underlying drivers of vulnerability, which may be beyond a single sector. For example, dealing with health impacts of climate change will entail solutions that tackle urban form, urban design, and urban health, thereby requiring interventions in spatial planning, infrastructure and housing, and public health. Strengthening the resilience of MSMEs also requires understanding local hazards as well as climate shocks and stresses that may impact the wider supply chain (e.g., droughts may impact agricultural production and thereby have an impact on urban MSME wholesalers and retailers of agricultural produce). Urban areas often span multiple districts, and thus an understanding of climate risk on the wider system will help ensure how resilience measures introduced in different

Understanding systems-level risks. Addressing the impacts of climate change on urban areas will require understanding the risks at the systems level and providing solutions that tackle urban form, urban design, and urban health.

parts of the area collectively contribute toward the resilience of the entire system. This will require enhanced coordination and improved governance. Understanding of such system-wide risks will also allow developing financial mechanisms to bridge actions at different scales.

Understanding the spatial and temporal nature of climate risk and how it interacts with urbanization and urban poverty to inform spending decisions. A comprehensive understanding of the spatial and temporal nature of climate risk, urbanization trend, and urban poverty, as well as their relationships, can support the national government in geographical targeting of financial flows, including climate finance. It can also help local governments identify risk and reflect adaptation priorities in local budgets. For example, with a higher proportion of poor and near-poor populations in non-metro areas, it might be useful to prioritize resilience-building interventions in such areas. The sheer recognition of the scale of risk and plausible impact will help foster partnerships with the private sector and communities in delivering resilience.

Integrating climate risk awareness in all capacity development programs. A key action would be to integrate climate risk topics in formal education curricula and capacity-building programs of government staff at national and local levels so that local governments are able to integrate climate change targets into the local planning and budgeting document or APBD. Similar awareness

raising should also be undertaken for the urban poor communities as part of various poverty reduction programs, such as family development sessions organized under social assistance programs, livelihood-related skill building programs targeted at the urban poor, training on operation and maintenance of community infrastructure, and community-level health awareness programs. Separate discussions should be conducted for women to raise their awareness and understand their needs and priorities. A key target would be facilitators of various poverty reduction programs who are involved in assisting local governments prepare project proposals for funding from national programs; socialization and community outreach activities; and monitoring of project implementation. Active use of the *Musrenbang* can be crucial for putting the spotlight on local climate risk issues and for strengthening coordination between different programs and local governments.

Investing in developing, maintaining, and integrating climate and disaster risk information with poverty and socioeconomic data. A key investment will be to align various datasets used for poverty reduction programs with climate and disaster risk databases, such as SIDIK and InaRISK. The former should capture information on poor and near-poor populations, the rate of in-migration, and the population dependent on the informal economy. These are critical for designing resilience solutions that can address the underlying drivers of vulnerabilities.

Ensuring Climate Policies Recognize the Importance of Addressing the Underlying Drivers of Vulnerability to Enable Transformational Adaptation

Factoring migration considerations in resilience interventions. Increasing extreme weather events, declining inhabitability of low-lying areas exposed to sea level rise, and shifts in natural resources can increase migration, including to urban areas. Indonesia is expected to be one of the first countries to experience "climate departure,"[116] which is likely to start as early as 2020 in Manokwari and by 2029 in Jakarta, substantially earlier than the world average of 2047.[117] The COVID-19 pandemic has also highlighted the need to consider migration-related issues in future resilience-building. Further efforts will be critical to understand potential climate-induced migration in Indonesia and how such an understanding can inform climate policies related to social protection, livelihoods, and housing. For example, it will be critical for social assistance programs to strengthen portability features that will allow poor households to carry their social assistance benefits when migrating from one part of the country to other to deal with lean periods of the year. Similarly, resilient livelihood programs should include the poor population who are engaged in the informal economy and who have migrated to urban areas to avoid the long-term impacts of climate change.

Adopting innovative approaches to address land tenure issues. Insecurity of land tenure is a key determinant of vulnerability among the urban poor. Lack of land tenure typically stops the urban poor households from receiving support from upgrading programs, makes formal access to basic services difficult, and also disincentivizes poor households to invest in resilience-building measures. Informal settlements lacking tenure only receive government support when they are affected by a government development project requiring relocation. However, for climate resilience targeted at the urban poor, addressing land tenure issues is critical because of its direct and indirect linkages with housing, basic services, and health. While difficult, successful examples of addressing land tenure with the support of community-led approaches have shown that it is possible to resolve land tenure issues at a city level, and that the local governments have the ability to act within the existing legal frameworks on land tenure, environmental management, and spatial development.[118] However, such approaches need to be institutionalized as a common approach to resolving tenure insecurity.

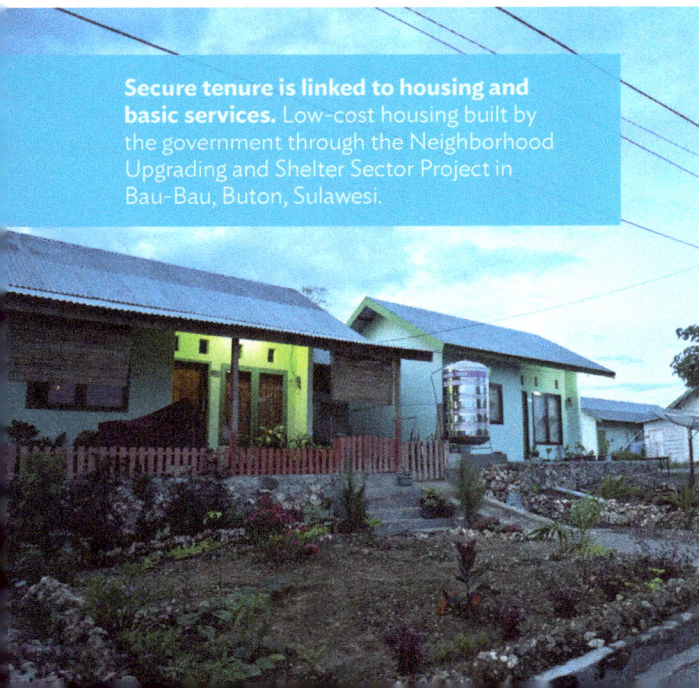

Secure tenure is linked to housing and basic services. Low-cost housing built by the government through the Neighborhood Upgrading and Shelter Sector Project in Bau-Bau, Buton, Sulawesi.

[116] It marks the point where climate begins to cease resembling what was before and moves into a new state.
[117] T. Fujii. 2016. *Climate Change and Vulnerability to Poverty: An Empirical Investigation in Rural Indonesia. ADBI Working Paper* 622. Tokyo: Asian Development Bank Institute.
[118] World Bank 2016. *Project Appraisal Document on a Proposed Loan for National Slum Upgrading Project.* Social, Urban, Rural and Resilience Global Practice East Asia and Pacific Region.

Scaling Up Investment in "No Regret" or "Low Regret" Solutions for Building Resilience of the Urban Poor

Scaling up investment in "no regret" or "low regret" solutions.[119] Limited understanding of future climate risk with its uncertainties, limited technical capacity and skills, and limited financial resources may make it difficult to always make a case for investing in stand-alone adaptation measures targeted at the urban poor. However, the focus could be on scaling up investments in "no regret" or "low regret" solutions that support reducing current climate risks while maintaining the flexibility to cope with future risks, thereby facilitating adaptation. These solutions provide benefits today and are robust against future uncertainty. Typically, such solutions involve enhanced management of natural resources and provision of public goods with co-benefits for adaptation. While these solutions do come at a cost, there is growing evidence on the cost-effectiveness of such investments and the dividend they produce. Most importantly, these solutions can be implemented through poverty reduction programs.

Investing in green infrastructure as part of urban poverty reduction programs. PBI 2020–2045 identifies the importance of green infrastructure in climate resilience — infrastructure built in harmony with the landscape or using environment-friendly and inexpensive technology for maintenance. Examples include urban agriculture and community gardens that help in soil water retention, urban tree cover in reducing urban temperature and surface runoff, restoration of urban waterways tackling rainwater drainage and stormwater control; and wetland protection, restoration of mangroves, and rehabilitation of coral reefs in coastal areas to protect against storm surges, coastal flood, and erosion. Studies show that nature-based solutions can be very effective for helping Jakarta deal with flood risk. Reducing runoff from rainfall by increasing vegetation in the high lands south of the city can help retain water upstream, and reduce hydraulic loads by providing more room for water and vegetation with green and blue spaces. A growing body of evidence shows that employing green infrastructure can achieve multiple goals that cut across livelihoods, sustainability, and resilience. While several initiatives, such as the Gerakan Pengurangan Resiko Bencana program, have been undertaken to promote green infrastructure, it is important that increased investments are made to take such solutions to scale. Existing poverty reduction programs across different sectors provide opportunities for green infrastructure solutions to scale. For example, the KOTAKU program can proactively promote water-sensitive urban landscape design and drainage system as part of neighborhood beautification processes. Employment generation programs in urban areas can promote mangrove protection, management of urban waterways, and urban agriculture. A further option is to explore innovative financing mechanisms, such as land value capture, payment for ecosystem services, reinvestment of dedicated green taxes, fees and charges, and climate finance to finance such measures by involving local governments, the private sector, CSOs, and communities.

Investing in integrated end-to-end early warning systems. The RPJMN 2020–2024 identifies investments in early warning systems as a priority for strengthening disaster resilience. Recent estimates show that investing $1.8 trillion globally in five climate adaptation areas, including strengthening early warning systems from 2020

---

[119] "No regret" and "low regret" solutions can be implemented regardless of climate change uncertainty as they reduce vulnerability to existing and future hazards and perform well across a range of climate change scenarios.

In harmony with the landscape. A path and drainage channel were built in the mangrove forest area of RW 09, Kelurahan Kesepuhan, Cirebon City.

to 2030, could generate $7.1 trillion in total new benefits.[120] The current COVID-19 crisis has highlighted the importance of improving preparedness to deal with shocks, be it health or other emergencies, and the important role integrated early warning systems can play. For example, early warning systems could include expanded use of ICT-based technologies to develop health early warning and surveillance systems that better predict health impacts of climate events, such as the link between temperature rise and heat-related mortality and morbidity or extreme rainfall and the spread of infectious disease. Seasonal forecasts provided by early warning systems can be used by city public works officials to plan the maintenance of urban infrastructure, such as cleaning drains, in order to ensure they function during disaster events, or by emergency management officials for pre-positioning of emergency supplies. Reliable weather forecasts become critical for providing triggers to horizontal and/or vertical expansion of social assistance programs, to operationalize business continuity plans of enterprises, and to activate community disaster preparedness plans. Moreover, the ways in which climate shocks and stresses affect the urban poor are not always direct. For example, they might present as food price increases (because of drought in rural areas) rather

than the loss of a dwelling or job. It is thus important to also track these broader effects as part of early warning systems in order to undertake *ex ante* interventions to assist the urban poor. The success of integrated early warning systems requires close collaboration with local governments and different sector ministries.

Implementing risk-sensitive spatial planning. Climate and disaster risk-informed spatial plans can bring transformational change by steering growth in non-hazard-prone areas, by promoting pro-poor urban forms that are sensitive to changes in future climate, introducing zoning ordinances that limit the exposure of urban poor to climate risk, and regulating the protection of urban ecosystems such as wetlands. Efforts undertaken to integrate climate change adaptation and disaster risk reduction into spatial planning process should be strengthened, and their implementation scaled up. This will require developing climate and disaster risk information (along with maps) at a scale appropriate for spatial planning, improving the capacity of local governments to undertake such assessments, and ensuring coordination among different agencies responsible for using the results of spatial plans for decision-making.

---

[120] Global Commission on Adaptation. 2019. *Adapt Now: A Global Call for Leadership on Climate Resilience*. Rotterdam.

Investing in New Programs for Building Resilience of the Urban Poor

Exploring the potential for developing a public work programs for employment generation. With increasing climate risk, large dependence on informal work among the urban poor, and expected increase in migration as a coping mechanism to deal with climate shocks and stresses, it will be important to explore the development of a national labor market program, such as labor-intensive public works programs. Many countries have successfully used such programs in providing cash to the poor and vulnerable households through cash for work scheme to rehabilitate small-scale infrastructure (e.g., canals) during lean periods and carry out reconstruction needs (e.g., site cleanup) after a disaster (footnote 42). They can also be key for building resilience by focusing on works with the primary purpose of protecting from climate shocks and stresses (e.g., drainage infrastructure), promoting nature-based solutions (e.g., protection of coastal mangroves), and enhancing skills in sustainable livelihoods (urban agriculture).

Establishing integrated resilience programs for outdoor urban workers. Outdoor workers are highly exposed to climate shocks and stresses, which impact their health and livelihoods. An integrated program on health, livelihoods, and infrastructure with explicit support on street vendors, street sweepers, and other outside workers can promote hydration regimes, introduce protocols for ventilation of workplaces, improve provision of public water fountains, and invest in outdoor infrastructure such as open sheds.

Introducing a dedicated program to support MSMEs build resilience. With a large percentage of the urban poor employed in MSMEs and their high levels of vulnerability (location specific as well as wider supply chain), it is important to introduce initiatives dedicated to building enterprise resilience. This is particularly true for MSMEs that are engaged and/or dependent on the sectors prioritized in PBI 2020–2045. Such an initiative could focus on (i) providing technical support to strengthen enterprise capacity in assessing climate and disaster risk in a range of aspects including selection of plant location, identification of key points in the supply chain and mapping of linkages within support organizations; (ii) supporting the development of long-term adaptation strategies; (iii) providing soft loans for enterprises to implement measures to reduce the risk on employees, infrastructure, stock, and supply chains; (iv) providing technical and financial support in managing the residual risk by implementing business continuity plans and improving access to credit and disaster insurance; and (v) linking enterprises with wider community disaster preparedness initiatives. Incentives can be formulated to encourage risk reduction measures, linking business continuity plans with criteria for access to credit or providing tax incentives for developing longer-term adaptation strategies. Certification schemes, awards, and recognition could also be provided.

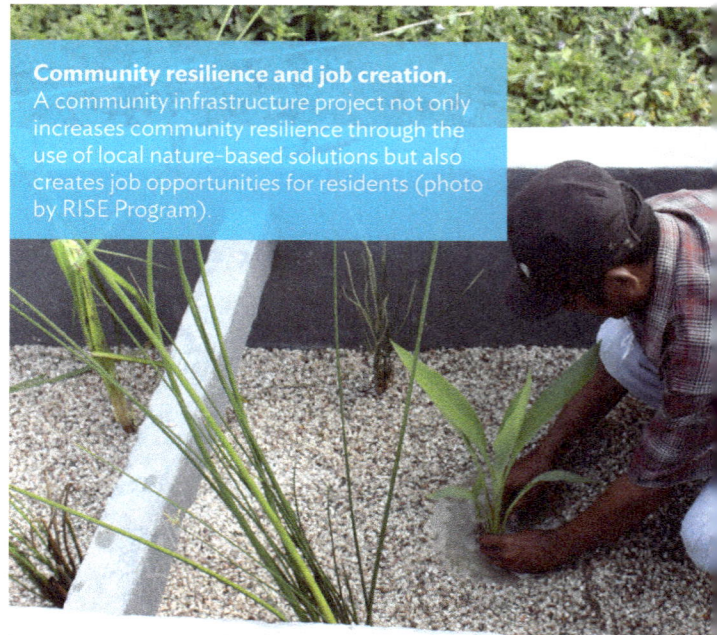

Community resilience and job creation. A community infrastructure project not only increases community resilience through the use of local nature-based solutions but also creates job opportunities for residents (photo by RISE Program).

Investing in Strengthening Financial Systems and Products to Promote Resilience of the Urban Poor

Strengthening public financial systems to support investments in resilience. Transformational adaptation requires long-term investments and the need to strengthen public financial management systems that allow allocating budget to support adaptation measures targeted at the urban poor. Such measures should include both capital expenditure and costs for operation and maintenance of community infrastructure, which will be impacted by changing hazard patterns. This will allow for infrastructure supported by national government agencies to be better maintained by subnational governments responsible for the day-to-day management and service delivery. A climate risk-informed public financial management system will allow allocation of DAK resources for poverty reduction to be guided by an understanding of risk and need for building resilience; promote the use of the Kelurahan Fund to finance strategic infrastructure needed for resilience-building, to introduce "no regret" solutions (as discussed earlier in the section), and to provide social assistance in a post-disaster context, as witnessed in the recent COVID-19 crisis; introduce incentives such as change-resilience conditions for the transfer of DID to local governments; and put in place systems to track adaptation finance to ensure funds are spent for appropriate activities that achieve value for money. Strengthened public financial management for climate resilience should also explore how adaptation finance can be delivered by a range of appropriate institutions, including local governments and CSOs, at appropriate volume, subsidiarity, and scale to meet local needs. It should also determine how national governments, regional government, municipalities, and external donors can combine finances to deliver on resilience objectives. Such systems also need to foster investments among the local private sector, communities,

Strengthening public financing to support community infrastructure. Using fiscal transfers for community infrastructure, such as health centers, has the potential to reduce vulnerability to climate impacts if informed by climate risk considerations.

and individual households to invest in resilience measures. Community participation is therefore required to ensure that any of the above actions are undertaken in ways that genuinely benefit the poor and maximize their impact. A strong directive from the National Budget Law (APBN) on climate adaptation targets will be critical to ensure public funding for resilience is mainstreamed in public budgets at national and local levels.

Strengthening systems to increase access of climate finance for adaptation priorities of the urban poor. It is important to work closely with Pusat Kebijakan Pendanaan Perubahan Iklim dan Multilateral (PKPPIM) to prioritize adaptation in climate finance allocation, especially for the urban areas, so that finance can be strategically used to unlock the potential for poverty reduction programs to deliver on resilience and to de-risk other forms of financing for resilience. A key priority will be to build capacity of urban local governments to access climate finance to implement priorities of the local climate adaptation plans and overcome barriers for resilience investments. It will be important to encourage international climate finance organizations to conduct better outreach programs for urban local governments on the potential to access such funds. Also important will be to partner with CSOs, such as slum and shack dwellers federations that have experience of managing finances, to explore the potential of channeling resources directly to the urban poor, where appropriate.

Developing innovative financial products for building resilience of the urban poor. While much can be done to build the resilience of the urban poor through the use of existing resources, and to some extent with support from climate finance, additional financing will also be required. Innovative approaches, such as through land-based fiscal tools or a green bond scheme, could be used to generate such financing. The Green Sukuk bonds[121] that have been issued in Indonesia are a good example of government innovation in leveraging private finance for green and sustainable development, and a similar model could be considered to support the resilience of the urban poor.[122] Innovative land-based fiscal tools, such as land value capture, could also be used to fund resilience measures targeted at the urban poor. For example, in cities with high climate and disaster risk, the impact of resilient infrastructure development can increase the land value, which can form the basis for taxes and thereby help recover the cost of investing in resilience. Other options to explore include blended finance, as currently seen in the One Million Houses Program, to mobilize private sector resources for investing in resilience. Partnerships with housing microfinance organizations can be explored to develop specific products to support low-income households with financial and technical support to repair, retrofit, and reconstruct housing. Another consideration could be strengthening the financial resilience of microfinance institutions by creating a contingent liquidity facility that they can draw from during disasters to meet the needs of their clients.

Developing innovative approaches that allow *ex ante* **access to humanitarian funding.** Worth exploring is the possibility of developing innovative financing mechanisms, such as forecast-based financing that allows local, national, and international humanitarian funding to be triggered based on robust forecasts and risk analysis. Such approaches can help reduce human suffering and the impacts of disasters. Such approaches can be linked to social assistance and livelihood programs and require robust early warning systems, clear protocols for trigger, and availability of liquidity.

---

[121] The Green Sukuk are Shari'ah-compliant investments in renewable energy and other environmental assets. In March 2018, the Ministry of Finance issued the very first sovereign Green Sukuk in United States dollars, raising $1.25 billion from a wide range of investors including green investors. The 5-year issuance was oversubscribed, showing the rising demand of investors for responsible and sustainable investments.
[122] C. Bauhet. 2018. Indonesia's Green Sukuk. United Nations Development Programme blog.

Conclusion

Building climate and disaster resilience is critical for the future of Indonesia. Without it, hard-won development gains will be lost, and people will be unable to escape from poverty. The economic benefits of urbanization will not be achieved and future hazards (including those associated with climate change) will continue to erode assets and cause injury and loss of life.

Building resilience. Indonesia's cities such as Cirebon have a role in implementing new programs dedicated for building resilience of the urban poor (photo by Barry Beagen).

Indonesia has robust national policies and programs spread across different sectors and targeted at the poor, including the urban poor. Five key policy areas include social protection, livelihoods, public health, housing, and community infrastructure. Programs in these policy areas provide opportunities for factoring in climate resilience strategies, especially where these programs directly or indirectly interact with priority adaptation sectors such as water, marine and coastal, agriculture, and health. The strategies could include a combination of coping mechanisms to deal with immediate risks, incremental adaptation to accommodate changes in climate, and transformational solutions that bring about fundamental systemic changes toward

reducing the root causes of vulnerability to climate change in the long run. Moreover, the scope of the programs allows targeting climate resilience strategies at different scales—household, community, cities, subnational, and national—with actions at any scale being complemented by activities and interventions at other scales.

Given the scale of climate risk the country faces, poverty reduction programs can effectively support climate resilience through additional climate investments in five key strategic areas. This includes (i) investing in strengthening awareness on future climate risk for urban poverty reduction; (ii) ensuring climate policies recognize

Figure 9: Applied Framework for Building Resilience of the Urban Poor

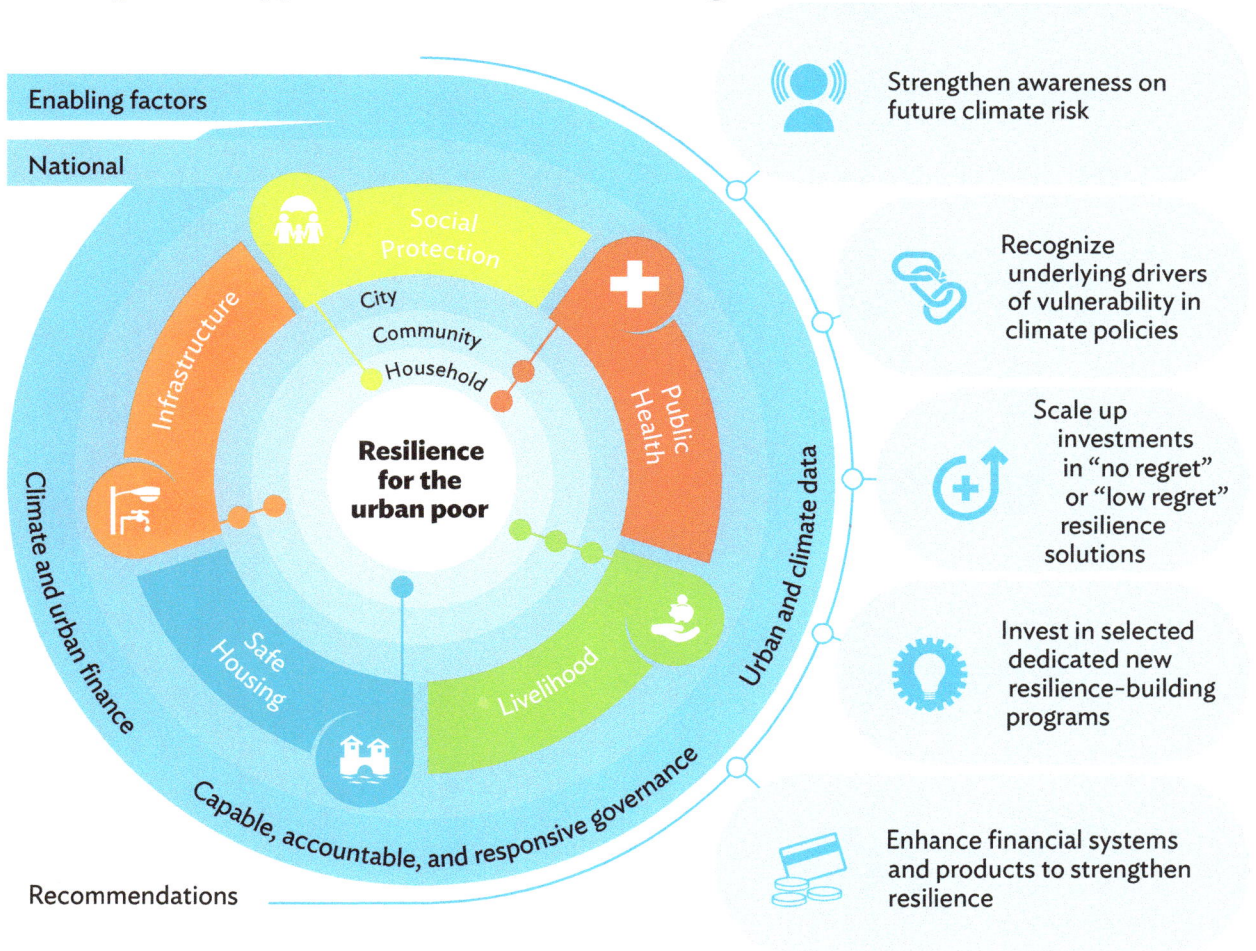

Source: Asian Development Bank.

the importance of addressing the underlying drivers of vulnerability for advancing climate resilience; (iii) scaling up investments in "no regret" or "low regret" solutions for building resilience; (iv) implementing programs dedicated for building resilience of the urban poor; and (v) investing in strengthening financial systems and products to promote resilience of the urban poor.

While individual actions are needed at the local level, the national government has a critical role through risk-informed and inclusive governance; generating, updating, and maintaining climate, disaster, and poverty data; and securing finance. These factors provide the enabling environment for securing and sustaining resilience and are also critical for facilitating innovation and partnerships necessary for scaling up resilience.

This approach of building resilience through poverty reduction policies and programs not only goes beyond merely reducing harm but also seeks to demonstrate how interventions to build resilience can address the underlying systemic factors in response to climate and its effects, and improve existing capacity, including acquiring new skills in the context of increasing climate and disaster risk. Such an approach will help to achieve the outcome of safe, inclusive, resilient, and sustainable urban development envisaged by the global Sustainable Development Goals and in line with the development goals in Indonesia's RPJMN 2020-2024 and PBI 2020-2045.

Additional References

Adani, N., and A. Maulana. 2019. What Happens to Poor Households: Are They Leaving, Staying or Falling? Evidence from Indonesia's Unified Database (UDB). *TNP2K Working Paper* 46/2019. Jakarta, Indonesia. http://tnp2k.go.id/downloads/what-happens-to-poor-households:-are-they-leaving,-staying-or-falling---evidence-from-indonesia%E2%80%99s-unified-database-(udb).

Aleksandrova, M. 2020. Principles and Considerations for Mainstreaming Climate Change Risk into National Social Protection Frameworks in Developing Countries. *Climate and Development.* Vol. 12 (6). https://www.tandfonline.com/doi/full/10.1080/17565529.2019.1642180.

Asian Development Bank. 2017. Completion Report: *Indonesia: Urban Sanitation and Rural Infrastructure Support to the PNPM Mandiri Project.* Manila. https://www.adb.org/sites/default/files/project-documents/43255/43255-013-pcr.pdf.

———. 2018. *Strengthening Resilience through Social Protection Programs: Guidance Note.* Manila. https://www.adb.org/sites/default/files/institutional-document/412011/resilience-social-protection-guidance-note.pdf

Asian Disaster Preparedness Center. 2016. *Strengthening Disaster and Climate Resilience of Small and Medium Enterprises in Asia: Indonesia.* https://app.adpc.net/sites/default/files/public/publications/attachments/1%20%20IP_Synthesis.pdf.

Banerjee, A., R. Hanna, B.A. Olken, E. Satriawan, and S. Sumarto. 2021. Food vs. Food Stamps: Evidence from an At-Scale Experiment in Indonesia. *Working Paper* 60-e-2021. The National Team for the Acceleration of Poverty Reduction and Australian Government. https://economics.mit.edu/files/21317.

Burger, N., P.J. Glick, F. Perez-Arce, L. Rabinovich, Y.R.L. Rana, S. Srinivasan, and J. Yoong. 2012. *Indonesia—Urban Poverty Analysis and Program Review* (English). World Bank Group. Washington, DC. http://documents.worldbank.org/curated/en/263151468275080963/Indonesia-Urban-poverty-analysis-and-program-review.

Cahaya, A. 2015. Fishermen Community in the Coastal Area: A Note from Indonesian Poor Family. *Procedia Economics and Finance.* Vol. 26. pp. 29–33. https://www.sciencedirect.com/science/article/pii/S2212567115008011.

Chaudhuri E., S. Kurniawati, and S. Sumarto. 2019. Decentralisation and Poverty Reduction: The Role of Local Economies and Institutional Capacity in Indonesia. *TNP2K Working Paper* 45-2019. Jakarta, Indonesia. http://tnp2k.go.id/downloads/decentralisation-and-poverty-reduction:-the-role-of-local-economies-and-institutional-capacity-in-indonesia.

City Form Lab. 2016. *Indonesia's Urban Story Exhibit.* http://cityformlab.org/projects/indonesia-s-urban-story-exhibit.

Climate Bonds Initiative. 2021. Green Sukuk.

du Toit, M.J., C.M. Shackleton, S.S. Cilliers, and E. Davoren.. 2021. Advancing Urban Ecology in the Global South: Emerging Themes and Future Research Directions. In C.M. Shackleton, S.S. Cilliers, E. Davoren, and M.J. du Toit, eds. *Urban Ecology in the Global South.* Cities and Nature. Cham, Switzerland: Springer. https://doi.org/10.1007/978-3-030-67650-6_17.

Faedlulloh, D., R. Prasetyanti, and B. Irawan. 2019. Kampung versus Climate Change: The Dynamics of Community Empowerment through the Climate Village Program (ProKlim). Journal of Physics: *Conference Series*. Vol. 1424. 012055. https://doi.org/10.1088/1742-6596/1424/1/012055.

Food and Agriculture Organization of the United Nations. 2008. *Climate Change and Food Security: A Framework Document*. http://www.fao.org/3/au035e/au035e.pdf.

Fujii, T. 2016. Climate Change and Vulnerability to Poverty: An Empirical Investigation in Rural Indonesia. *ADBI Working Paper* 622. Tokyo: Asian Development Bank Institute. https://www.adb.org/publications/climate-change-vulnerability-poverty-indonesia.

Gibson, L. 2017. Towards a More Equal Indonesia: How the Government Can Take Action to Close the Gap Between the Richest and the Rest. *Oxfam Briefing Paper* (February). https://policy-practice.oxfam.org/resources/towards-a-more-equal-indonesia-how-the-government-can-take-action-to-close-the-620192/.

Government of Indonesia. 2016. *First Nationally Determined Contributions: Republic of Indonesia*. https://www4.unfccc.int/sites/ndcstaging/PublishedDocuments/Indonesia%20First/First%20NDC%20Indonesia_submitted%20to%20UNFCCC%20Set_November%20%202016.pdf.

Government of Indonesia, Ministry of Environment and Forestry. 2014. *Program Kampung Iklim (ProKlim): Local Action to Respond [to] Climate Change*. 3rd Annual Meeting of the LoCARNet Presentation. November 2014. Indonesia. https://lcs-rnet.org/pdf/lcs_rnet_presentations/6th/P2.D-2_Suryanti.pdf.

———. 2015. *Climate Change Adaptation Policy and Programs in Indonesia*. PowerPoint presentation. http://copjapan.env.go.jp/cop/cop21/program/151207/1515-1715/pdf/cop21-jp-151207-1515-1715-presentation-02.pdf.

———. 2019. *Low Carbon Development: A Paradigm Shift Towards a Green Economy in Indonesia (Policymakers' Summary)*. https://drive.bappenas.go.id/owncloud/index.php/s/7flusfQXEdx4tmG#pdfviewer.

———. 2019. *National Adaptation Plan Executive Summary 2019*. https://lcdi-indonesia.id/wp-content/uploads/2020/05/Executive-Summary-NAP.pdf.

———. 2021. *Climate Change Can Disrupt the Economy* (5 April 2021)https://lcdi-indonesia.id/2021/04/05/bappenas-perubahan-iklim-dapat-mengganggu-perekonomian/.

———. 2021. *Climate Resilience Development Policy 2020–2045*. https://lcdi-indonesia.id/wp-content/uploads/2021/04/Buku-0_Ringkasan-Eksekutif-Dokumen-Kebijakan-Pembangunan-Berketahanan-Iklim.pdf.

———. n.d. *Poverty Reduction Programs in Indonesia*. https://www.bappenas.go.id/files/7213/8070/7102/Poverty_Reduction_Program_in_Indonesia.pdf.

Government of Indonesia, Ministry of National Development Planning (BAPPENAS). 2015. *Social Protection to Reduce Poverty in Indonesia*. PowerPoint presentation 10 April 2015. Jakarta. http://inahea.org/files/hari3/Vivi%20Yulaswati%20-%20Bappenas%20-%20Social%20Protection%20to%20Reduce%20Poverty%20in%20Indonesia.pdf.

Government of Indonesia, Ministry of Public Works and Public Housing. 2017. *KOTAKU Program Information Handbook At A Glance*. http://kotaku.pu.go.id/view/6980/handbook-sekilas-informasi-program-kotaku.

Government of Indonesia, National Team for the Acceleration of Poverty Reduction (TNP2K). 2014. *Reaching Indonesia's Poor and Vulnerable and Reducing Inequality: Improving Programme Targeting, Design, and Processes.* http://www.tnp2k.go.id/images/uploads/downloads/Report_REACHING_Mar30_LR.pdf.

———. 2018. *The Future of the Social Protection System in Indonesia: Social Protection for All.* http://www.developmentpathways.co.uk/wp-content/uploads/2018/11/44293181123-SP-ReportFinal-ENG-web.pdf.

———. 2018. Urban Village Fund (Dana Kelurahan) Allocation, Formulation, and Utilisation. *TNP2K Policy Brief.* http://tnp2k.go.id/downloads/urban-village-fund--(dana-kelurahan)-allocation,-formulation,-and-utilisation.

Hecht, J. 2016. *Indonesia: Costs of Climate Change 2015.* Technical Report. United States Agency for International Development. https://www.climatelinks.org/resources/indonesia-costs-climate-change-2050-technical-report.

Hidayati, D., *et al.* 2017. *Assessing the National Action Plan for Inclusive Policy Design of Climate Change Adaptation in Indonesia's Coastal Areas.* Jakarta: LIPI. http://www.unesco.or.id/publication/Laporan_Final_English_ActionPlanClimateChange.pdf.

Islamic Development Bank. 2019. A Decade of Action: Positioning IsDB Group to Meaningfully Contribute to the 2030 Agenda. *SDGs Digest.* Issue No. 9. https://www.isdb.org/sites/default/files/media/documents/2020-08/SDGs%20Digest%20ISSUE%20NO.9.pdf.

Lestari, E., C.A. Makarim, and W.A. Pranoto. 2019. *Zero Run-Off Concept Application in Reducing Water Surface Volume.* https://iopscience.iop.org/article/10.1088/1757-899X/508/1/012019/pdf.

Mills, F., J. Willetts, and M. Al Afghani. 2017. Increasing Local Government Responsibility for Communal Scale Sanitation. Part 1: Review of National Program Guidelines and Two City Case Studies. *Indonesia Infrastructure Initiative.* https://opus.lib.uts.edu.au/bitstream/10453/122064/1/lg-responsibilitycommunalscalesanitationpart-1.pdf.

Nelson, D.R., M.C. Lemos, H. Eakin, and Y.-J. Lo. 2016. The Limits of Poverty Reduction in Support of Climate Change Adaptation. *Environmental Research Letters.* Vol. 11 (9). https://iopscience.iop.org/article/10.1088/1748-9326/11/9/094011.

Organisation for Economic Co-operation and Development. 2018. Climate-Resilient Infrastructure. *OECD Environment Policy Papers* No. 14. Paris. https://www.oecd-ilibrary.org/docserver/4fdf9eaf-en.pdf?expires=1632115848&id=id&accname=guest&checksum=4645E40C704AA72AB05F0F65080A813D.

Ranger, N., and S. Garbett-Shiels. 2011. *How Can Decision-Makers in Developing Countries Incorporate Uncertainty About Future Climate Risks into Existing Planning and Policymaking Processes.* https://www.lse.ac.uk/granthaminstitute/publication/how-can-decision-makers-in-developing-countries-incorporate-uncertainty-about-future-climate-risks-into-existing-planning-and-policymaking-processes/.

Roberts, M., F. Gil Sander, and S. Tiwari. 2019. *Time to ACT: Realizing Indonesia's Urban Potential.* World Bank. Washington, DC. https://openknowledge.worldbank.org/handle/10986/31304.

Schneider, S. 2003. Abrupt Non-Linear Climate Change, Irreversibility and Surprise. *Working Paper.* Organisation for Economic Co-operation and Development. https://www.oecd.org/environment/cc/2482280.pdf.

SMERU Research Institute. 2008. The Specific Allocation Fund (DAK): Its Mechanisms and Uses. *SMERU Newsletter* No. 25 (January–April). http://www.smeru.or.id/sites/default/files/publication/news25.pdf.

United Nations Development Programme Indonesia. 2017. *The Role of Zakat in Supporting the Sustainable Development Goals*. https://www.id.undp.org/content/indonesia/en/home/library/sustainable-development-goals/the-role-of-zakat-in-supporting-the-sustainable-development-goal.html.

Water Environment Partnership in Asia (WEPA). 2013. Community-based Sanitation Lessons Learned from SANIMAS Programme in Indonesia. *WEPA Policy Briefs Series* 2 (March) http://www.wepa-db.net/pdf/1403policy_brief/WEPA_PB2_2013.pdf.

Wilhelm, M. 2011. The Role of Community Resilience in Adaptation to Climate Change: The Urban Poor in Jakarta, Indonesia. In: K. Otto-Zimmermann (eds). *Resilient Cities. Local Sustainability*. Vol. 1. Dordrecht, Netherlands: Springer. https://doi.org/10.1007/978-94-007-0785-6_5.

World Bank. 2006. *Making the New Indonesia Work for the Poor*. Washington, DC. https://openknowledge.worldbank.org/handle/10986/8172.

———. 2011. Jakarta *Urban Challenges in a Changing Climate*. Washington, D.C. https://documents1.worldbank.org/curated/en/132781468039870805/pdf/650180WP0Box360ange0Jakarta0English.pdf.

———. 2013. Indonesia : *Evaluation of the Urban Community Driven Development Program, Program Nasional Pemberdayaan Masyarakat Mandiri Perkotaan*. Washington, DC. https://openknowledge.worldbank.org/handle/10986/17870.

———. 2013. Indonesia : *Urban Poverty and Program Review*. Washington, DC. https://openknowledge.worldbank.org/handle/10986/16301.

———. 2013. *Urban Sanitation Review: Indonesia Country Study*. Washington, DC. https://openknowledge.worldbank.org/handle/10986/17614.

———. 2015. *PAMSIMAS - Responding to the Water and Sanitation Challenges in Rural Indonesia*. Washington, D.C. http://documents.worldbank.org/curated/en/938961468195535278/PAMSIMAS-Responding-to-the-water-and-sanitation-challenges-in-Rural-Indonesia.

———. 2020. *Indonesia Public Expenditure Review (Chapter 10: Housing)*. https://pubdocs.worldbank.org/en/704221590233780563/ID-PER-2020-Ch10-Housing.pdf.

———. 2020. KOTAKU Program Supports Response to COVID-19 Outbreak in 364 Urban Villages (Kelurahan). *Bicara Bencana*. Issue 02 (May 2020).

World Bank Group and Asian Development Bank. 2021. Climate Risk Profile: Indonesia. https://www.adb.org/sites/default/files/publication/700411/climate-risk-country-profile-indonesia.pdf.

World Health Organization. 2015. *Operational Framework for Building Climate Resilient Health Systems*. https://www.who.int/globalchange/publications/building-climate-resilient-health-systems/en.

www.ingramcontent.com/pod-product-compliance
Lightning Source LLC
Chambersburg PA
CBHW061220270326
41926CB00032B/4794

* 9 7 8 9 2 9 2 6 9 1 0 2 8 *